LIVING LIFE
God's Way

LIVING LIFE
God's Way

PETER HORROBIN

Sovereign World Ltd
Bringing together the Word & the Spirit

Sovereign World Ltd
PO Box 784
Ellel
Lancaster LA1 9DA
England

www.sovereignworld.com

ISBN 978-1-85240-758-2

Printed in the United Kingdom

Contents

Acknowledgements

Many different people have contributed to *Living Life God's Way* – but most are not even aware of the part they have played! In reality every single person who has impacted my life has contributed to the person I am and helped me to understand something of what God intended life to be.

Many of the stories in this book relate to my childhood upbringing – I will be eternally grateful to my parents for all I learnt from them about life and about God. My children, members of the wider family, colleagues in work, fellow members of many different churches and the wider Christian community have all had a significant part to play.

My fellow leaders in the work of Ellel Ministries and members of the teams at all the Ellel centers have made vital contributions to the pilgrimage. As have many different advisers such as Jim Graham, who so generously contributed the Foreword to the book.

Many others have helped with the compilation, reading, editing and publishing of *Living Life God's Way* – I am deeply grateful to each and every one.

I am especially grateful, however, to my wife Fiona, with whom so much of what this book contains has been shared in the day-to-day reality of living the Christian life. Those closest to you always bear the biggest cost of producing a book!

Above all I give thanks to God my Savior, without whom real life would be impossible.

Foreword by Jim Graham

This book embodies a heart-cry to get back to basics in Christianity. It is a solid, secure, Bible-based book that is a stable foundation for Christian living in its original and continuing sense.

Peter, in his writing, betrays a keen mind which is not content simply with ideas or concepts but is determined to put flesh on the bones of theology and shoes on its feet. He brings to the task the clear, clinical eye of the scientist; the problem-solving creativity of the engineer; the warm, compassionate heart of the disciple of Christ; the sensitive spirit of the pastor who never became a Pastor; and the risk-taking faith of the spiritual entrepreneur often living on the edge of vision.

The four most fundamental questions that face everyone, without exception, are confronted and then addressed in a practical and biblical way in *Living Life God's Way*.

These four questions are:

1. Where did I come from?

Am I simply a higher animal with all the implications of that for living and dying? Or did I come from God's creative hand? Do I have the dignity and distinctiveness of having been made to resemble God? Is human life special and precious? The consequence of answering that question, with authority, has a massive impact not only on human history but also on human destiny.

2. Who am I?

Is man simply, as William Shakespeare affirms, *"Dressed in a little brief authority; most ignorant of what he is most assured. His glassy essence, like an angry ape, plays such fantastic tricks before high heaven as makes the angels weep"*? Is he, as Pascal exclaims, *"What a chimera is man then? What a novelty, what a monster, what a chaos, what a subject of contradiction, what a prodigy! Judge of all things, imbecile, earthworm, depository of the truth, sewer of uncertainty and error, glory and refuse of the universe"*? Or am I a sinner corrupted and seduced by the selfishness of my humanity; a victim of destructive temptation; and yet pursued relentlessly by the redeeming and creative love of God?

3. Why am I here?

Have I been born simply as the result of a physical act? Do I live to no purpose? Will I die with no hope? Is life simply a meaningless absurdity? Or am I here to broker the unseen into the seen? Is there something of heaven that is born within me while I am still on earth that needs to be released through me? Am I in a position to allow God to flow through me so that the geography around me will forever be changed? Have I been born to discover a living and vibrant relationship with a holy God and then to demonstrate the reality of that relationship among those with whom I have contact?

4. What is my destiny?

Was the twentieth-century philosopher Bertrand Russell right when he said, *"When I die I shall rot, and nothing of my soul shall survive…There is darkness without and when I die there will be darkness within. There is no splendour, no vastness anywhere; only triviality for a moment, and then nothing"?* Was Tom Stoppard terrifyingly right when he said, *"Death is not anything…death is not…it's the absence of presence, nothing more…The endless time of never coming back. A gap you can't see, and when the wind blows through it, it makes no sound"?* Or am I bound for the land of the living having left the land of the dying? Am I destined to inherit a new heaven and a new earth, with a new body, where there is service without weariness; life without death; joy without sorrow; light without darkness; glory without suffering; living without sinning; and presence without absence?

No wonder the apostle Paul writes to the Ephesian Christians (in what is probably a circular letter!), as paraphrased here from Chapter 4:

> *So far this letter has been about two things. First, the astounding, amazing, extravagant grace of God for all who will respond to it whatever their background. Second, that this God would want someone like me, of all people, to be made aware of this and then to share it with others. Because of this I have landed up in prison.*
>
> *However, that brings me to the third reason for writing this letter – that this sheer, undeserved generosity of God needs to have shoes on its feet and clothes on its back so that it can be seen and understood in the real world. Truth believed needs to be truth behaved otherwise it is not really truth believed.*
>
> *Unless this truth radically and intrusively affects our life-style and the way we live, it is completely irrelevant and utterly useless. So, hear the longing and yearning of my heart that you would take this seriously and be completely different people from what you used to be. How are you to do this? By stopping all your attempts at trying to be good*

and letting God do what He wants to do both in you and
through you.

This is a revolutionary and comprehensive life-change and
does not come easily to any of us because of our proud hearts.
We need consciously and deliberately to move over from the
driving seat of our lives and allow God to be responsible for
the direction we now take...

That is precisely what *Living Life God's Way* is all about. It
has a firm, understandable, biblical base and then goes on to
give clear directions about how to feed the new life of God
that has been born within us and express its reality in practical
terms.

I have no doubt that it will be translated into other languages,
so that it will be a vital tool to help stabilize and mature the
stunning growth of the Church around the world. And for the
present it will be an investment now in the life of the believer
(*I found something happened to my own walk with Jesus as I read the*
manuscript) as he/she addresses the basic beliefs of the Christian
Faith and the consequent behavior that understanding and
integrity demands.

It is probably unhelpful to be selective in a book of this kind
but I did find Chapters 6, 8, 9, 10, 13 and 15 to be particularly
helpful practically, in an "in your face" way!

There is another way, also, in which this book could be of
enormous value. Across the United Kingdom there is a growing
awareness that older Christians need to take responsibility to
care for and mentor those who have been *not-yet-Christians* and
are now *just-become-Christians*. I cannot think of a better text-
book to use in this process than *Living Life God's Way*. It would
not be a question of "buy one, and get one free" but rather buy
two – and use one freely to help grow a new man or woman
of God!

I pray that as you use this book it will help you to be a Kingdom person and help others to become Kingdom people too.

Jim Graham
Pastor Emeritus,
Gold Hill Baptist Church,
Buckinghamshire, UK

Please note:

The paraphrase from Ephesians Chapter 4, is from Jim Graham's own personalized translation of Paul's epistles, published by Sovereign World as The God-Life in 2016.

This shortened version of Jim Graham's Foreword first appeared in the original edition of this book published in 2008.

Preface

The first time I went canoeing, the inevitable happened! There was a collision, I lost my balance and the next thing I remember was hanging upside down, from the canoe, under the water. I am a tall man, my legs are long and for a few seconds I couldn't extract them from the capsized canoe. I was trapped.

Suddenly my legs came free, my life-jacket did its job, and, much to my relief, my head popped up above the water. The crisis was over. Even though there were expert life-savers around and, I am told, there was no critical danger, nothing could take away from me the thought that for a few seconds I was not just suspended from a canoe – but I was suspended between life and death!

The consequences of death are only fully appreciated when the possibility of dying stares you in the face. But when the crisis is over the ordinary activities of life very quickly regain their day-to-day significance. We don't like to think too long or too hard about the fact of death. But, in life, bodily death is the only thing we can look forward to with absolute certainty!

So, when Jesus told His followers, *"I have come that you might have life – life in all its fullness,"* He was speaking about a subject which is of vital concern to every single person. For life is the only antidote to death. And for all who know Jesus, death is no longer an enemy to be feared but a gateway to a new life. Passing through that gateway – from death to life – is undoubtedly the most important journey anyone can ever take.

The original edition of this book was written in support of *Mission England*, the great evangelistic campaign that was conducted in the United Kingdom by Billy Graham. That mission was a milestone in my own life. Many lifelong friendships were established as we worked together for the mission. I am still today involved with the regular compilation of new editions of *Mission Praise*, the hymn and song-book which was conceived and birthed through the mission. And some of the relationships established at that time were strategic in the foundation of Ellel Ministries, which has been my own life's calling for thirty years and more.

Hope and Healing

Ellel Ministries was founded to bring hope and healing to the hurting. It quickly grew into a teaching and discipling ministry and now there are over thirty Ellel Centers around the world proclaiming the truth of Luke 9:11 – that Jesus still welcomes people, is still wanting them to learn the truths of His Kingdom and is still wanting them to be healed!

As week by week new groups of people came on the Healing Retreats and training courses at Ellel Grange, initially from the North-West of England, then from the whole country and before long from around the world, I was profoundly impacted by how few of the people who came for help actually understood what living the Christian life is meant to be. Most had been churchgoers all their lives, but the basic principles of Christian living did not seem to have been fully appreciated.

Most who came knew about God and had a basic understanding of the fundamentals of Christian truth, but it had never dawned upon many of them that they could actually know God for themselves. Many knew God in the sense that they could remember a time when they became a Christian and they were expecting that when they died they would go to heaven, but the idea that there was a dynamic Kingdom life to be lived here on earth had somehow escaped their understanding! And the majority were unaware of any possible connection between their personal circumstances, the way they lived and their need for healing.

I thought back to my own years of involvement in various evangelistic initiatives and many years of listening to sermons in churches of varying colors and flavors. I realized how little of the teaching was probably relevant to the day-to-day issues of life. For most church-going people the idea of going to heaven when you die was an important belief, because it provided great comfort to the dying. But the practical application of being a Christian, summarized by the words of Jesus when He said, *"if you love me you will obey me,"* seemed not to be of particular significance – even though the relationship between love and obedience is the very essence of Christian discipleship!

It is so easy when involved in evangelism to focus all one's attention on the need to help people into the Kingdom of God, and forget that unless those who have entered the Kingdom of God are given a guide and a guidebook to the territory, they will soon get lost and wonder what it's all about! There are many people in the world who have tried Christianity in this way, but have not found many of life's major questions being answered and have quickly returned to depending on their own wisdom and before very long have become casualties of the Church.

There was a time when I had to go through my own personal repentance over this issue, realizing that bringing a person to faith in Christ and then telling them that when they die they will now go to heaven, was not the whole gospel! Not that I have changed in my understanding that the first step of salvation is important – it is of critical importance. Nor have I changed in

my belief as to what happens to a believer when they die! But I
have additionally grown to realize the importance of what Jesus
encouraged us to believe for, in the Lord's Prayer, when He told
us to pray that the Kingdom of God would come here on earth.
And that has become the focus of the rest of my life – seeking
not only to help people into the Kingdom, but teach them what
Living Life God's Way as a child of the King really means.

It is the experience of living in the Kingdom of God here
on earth which is largely absent from much of the Church
and, dare I say, is probably responsible for the wholesale
collapse in traditional church-going by those who have never
comprehended that becoming a Christian is not only receiving
the gift of salvation, but choosing to live under a new Kingdom
authority.

The Reason for the Book

And so to the reason for this book – it is not just a book about
becoming a Christian, it is about *living the life* of a Christian. In
it I draw on many years of experience in seeking to encourage
people forward in their relationship with God, understanding
that a primary definition of both discipleship and healing is
simply *the restoration of God's order in a person's life*. Where
there is disorder, there is potential for chaos! And many of
the difficulties people encounter in life have their origin in the
unresolved disorder that can often dominate their day-to-day
activities.

The chapters have been organized into eighteen different top-
ics. An 18-part DVD series and Study Guide is also available, under
the title *"Life is for Living"*. Each 26 minute video expands on what
is in the book. Both the book and the DVD series are complete in
themselves. However, when taken together they make an ideal

series of discipleship training programs for small group meetings in the local church.

We begin the book by looking at the foundational beliefs (the doctrines) of the Christian faith. Please don't think these are unimportant or boring – they are critical, life-changing and essential to our spiritual survival!

Paul urged the young leader Timothy to guard his doctrine. If Timothy was to believe wrong things it would have catastrophic outworkings in his life and ministry. The Captain of the *Titanic* believed his ship was unsinkable and that no iceberg could interrupt the progress of the great ship. This was a wrong belief (*a wrong doctrine!*) – it led to the loss of the ship and thousands of lives!

I pray that as you read the book you will allow God to challenge and encourage you to believe the Truth and live the Life that God has called you to. And then experience the greatest joy this world has to offer, as you discover your destiny in God.

Peter Horrobin
Ellel Grange, January 2017

CHAPTER 1

WHO IS GOD? AND WHAT'S HE LIKE?

The God Box

All of life is a learning experience. From the moment we are conceived, through our developmental months to that moment of birth and throughout our growing years, even to the very end of our days, we are constantly storing away knowledge that is gained through experience. Additionally, we can read, study and learn from the experiences and knowledge gained by others in a continuing process of education and personal training.

And just as we spend much of our lives acquiring bits of information about the world and how to live in it, we are also acquiring bits of spiritual information that go into a special place in our understanding which I shall call the *God box*.

All of us are primarily spiritual beings. In the earliest days of our life, from conception onwards, it is our spirit that is most alert to what is going on around us. Our spirit is very sensitive to things which are spiritual. All of us have many spiritual experiences, and, almost without thinking, we put these experiences in the *God box* and store them up for future use – both the good ones and the bad ones.

It was God's intention that we should all learn about Him through godly parents, who brought us up in the love and nurture of the Lord. But reality for most people has been a long way from the ideal and not all our experiences have been good and not every spiritual experience we have had has actually been about God!

Some have been brought up to believe the name of God or Jesus is simply a convenient swear word, to use when under pressure and you don't know what else to say! Many have been brought up to believe that God doesn't exist. Many others have been brought up in religions that talk about "God," but which, in reality, are leading people into a false spiritual understanding. As a result the information in our *God box* usually falls a long way short of what we need to know, in order to make even the most basic decisions about life.

I once had a favorite jigsaw puzzle. I loved this particular puzzle, but after it had been lent to a friend, it was returned with some pieces missing. Without those pieces the picture was incomplete. On another occasion I brought back from overseas a particularly difficult jigsaw puzzle for my son. It was called an Impossi-puzzle because, in addition to all the real pieces that made up the jigsaw, there were also some extra pieces which looked like the real thing but which did not fit at all into the jigsaw.

In life the *God box* that most people carry around with them is a bit like a combination of the above two jigsaws. There are pieces missing from their understanding about God and they have also acquired quite a lot of spiritual information, which they think is about God, but which in reality is nothing to do with God at all!

With this being the real scenario for so many people's lives, it is hardly surprising that they are living with an inadequate spiritual foundation and are suffering many of the consequences of having made life's choices without having enough knowledge about what God is really like. When you shake out the pieces of their jigsaw from the *God box*, you discover that there is both a lot missing and a lot there that shouldn't be there. And this is true for many, if not most, of the people who are struggling with trying to live the Christian life.

It is impossible to help people to live the Christian life, unless they are building on a good foundation. For this reason, the first few chapters of this book are designed to help you look again at what you know about God in the light of the truth, as it has been revealed in and through the life of Jesus.

You may think that you know all this already, and as a result will want to skip the first few chapters, but may I encourage you to work through the chapters carefully, one at a time. You may be very surprised at what you discover, both about yourself and about God. Reading these few chapters alone could be a life-changing experience for you.

I have spent most of the past thirty years helping people bring godly order into their lives through a process of healing and discipleship in the work of Ellel Ministries. Time and again I have discovered that people who thought they knew everything they needed to know about Christian truth, in reality knew a lot less than was necessary for godly living. It was often no surprise, therefore, to discover how wrong beliefs had led them into wrong choices and now, years later, they were struggling with all the consequences of not having a *God box* filled with truth.

So Who is God?

Throughout history human beings have constantly asked questions about the existence of God and, if He exists, what is He like? Common sense says that this amazing world, in which we live, could not have appeared out of nothing. Common sense, therefore, says that there must be a creator. And just as there cannot be more than one potter turning a pot on the wheel, there cannot be more than one creator of this extraordinary universe. And if there is only one Creator of the universe, then He alone must be God and there is only one God.

Everything we are must have come from God. He is not only the Creator of the physical universe in which we live and move and have our being, but He is also the source of life itself. We are, ultimately, totally dependent on Him.

The logic behind this simple argument is devastatingly simple, but, sadly, far too simple for some of the great men of science who have devoted their minds and their lives to trying to prove the irrelevance of the very idea of God! Yet many of the greatest early pioneers in science were Christians. It was their very faith in God which led them to explore the universe to discover, not just the truth about God, but the truth about the universe that God had made.

Ultimately, there is no conflict between science and theology or science and faith. Science sets out to discover the truth about every single aspect of the universe we live in. The faith community also wants to discover the truth. Astronomers study the extent of the universe, chemists study what it is made of, doctors study how our bodies work and theologians study the God who made it all. All of them are united in this one objective, the discovery of truth. And when great scientific discoveries are made, the world honors the scientists who have added further knowledge to the catalogue of human achievement. *Nobel Prizes* are awarded to those who make the greatest discoveries.

Conversely, the nature of man – as opposed to the nature of his physical body – and the nature of God are not measurable by scientific instruments. When we ask questions, therefore, about *Who is God?* and we want to know *What is He Like?* we are entering the realm of faith. But the goal of both the scientific community and the faith community is ultimately the same –

the discovery of truth. Both know that it is only truth that will satisfy. But what is truth? The whole of history hinges on that very question.

What is Truth?

A prisoner stood before a Roman provincial governor. In response to the prisoner's statement that he had *"come to testify to the truth,"* Pontius Pilate responded with a rhetorical question, to which Pilate did not believe there was an answer. *"What is truth?"* he said, as he turned away, not waiting for a response from the prisoner.

Little did Pilate realize that standing before him was the very embodiment of truth and the only meaningful point of harmony between science and faith. Here was the physical presence and tangible body of a man who was also the ultimate demonstration of the truth about God. In Him, science and faith meet, and scientists and believers can discover that they are both on the same side of the fence when they realize that in Jesus there is a unique point of convergence, where *truth divine (in the spirit)* and *truth incarnate (in the flesh)* meet.

In the world of science truth is arrogant. It does not accept compromise. There cannot be two truths which are mutually at odds with each other. Gravity cannot have two different values. Water cannot be made up of two atoms of hydrogen and one of oxygen in one place, and have a different constitution in a different place. A substance with a different constitution is no longer water.

Science depends on the un-changeability of truth. If supposed facts are variable, then something is wrong. They are no longer facts, but competing theories. Everything we use in this technological world depends on the unchangeability of scientific truth – facts are facts and cannot be altered.

I am writing this book on a computer which has been pro-
grammed to convert the movements of my fingers on a keyboard into letters appearing on a screen. I depend on all those
hidden processes being unchanging. When I press the letter T,
I expect a T to appear on the screen. If the keyboard was constantly and randomly changing, typing even one word would
become impossible. Every time we fly in a plane we depend on
the unchangeability of gravity. If gravity varied flying would be
impossible. The laws of science are the fundamental building
bricks of the material world in which we live and on which we
depend for so much.

But if the world in which we live is governed by unchangeable laws (which it is) and we believe in a Creator, who is
God, then we also believe in a God who is a God of order and
discipline, who put those unchangeable laws (truth about the
world) into place. He must also be the origin of unchangeable
truth, the source of all knowledge and the very foundation of
science itself. Indeed, the very word "science" simply means
knowledge.

It is a fact that unchangeable physical laws describe the universe. They describe what keeps the stars in place and our own
earth in orbit around the sun. They describe the movement
of the tides and everything God made - the seas, the land and
everything in it. And these unchangeable laws are simply a consequence of the intrinsic nature of matter, out of which everything
is made!

It seems strange to me that the world of science, which rec-
ognizes and promotes the truth about the unchangeable nature
of matter in the physical world, seems reluctant to recognize that
there are equally important spiritual truths and spiritual laws
at work, which are also unchangeable. These spiritual laws are
truths which have their origin in God, just as much as the physical laws of matter have their origin in their Creator!

In the Bible, Jesus talked about spiritual Laws that would stay in place until the end of all things. In Matthew 5:17 Law has a capital L in most Bibles, which would indicate that these Laws come from God and are not man's ideas. When Moses brought two tablets of stone down from the mountain top, on which had been written the Ten Commandments by the finger of God, God was not just giving the Children of Israel some practical notes for daily living. He was giving mankind an understanding of how we should live if we do not want to discover the unchangeable spiritual laws of the spiritual universe the hard way! Commandments are there for our safety and well-being – not as a restriction on the enjoyment of life.

If you ignore the danger sign saying **"DANGER – Do not proceed beyond this point"** (the commandment) and walk off the edge of a high cliff, you will discover the law of gravity the hard way. If you ignore the sign by the electrified railway track, which warns of the danger of touching the live rail (the commandment), you will die as you discover a law of electricity the hard way. Similarly, if you swallow poison, you will discover some of the laws of chemistry the hard way.

Our world is full of warning signs (commandments) that have been put there to warn us of danger – they don't tell us which scientific laws we will discover if we ignore the warning, they just tell us it's dangerous to our physical well-being and expect us to take note of the warning for our own good. And there is no doubt that if we disobey these very practical commandments we will discover these laws the hard way.

In just the same way, when God gave us the Ten Commandments, He was not trying to deprive us of fun, but warning us of things which are dangerous to our spiritual health and, consequently, to our whole well-being. He didn't tell us which spiritual laws we would discover the hard way if we disobeyed them, but it is not hard to work them out. Later on we will return to take a closer look at the Ten Commandments, God's guidelines for healthy living.

Summary

God is the Creator of everything that exists. He is also the origin of truth, and the truth about God and His creation is as unvariable and as absolute as the laws of science. It is obvious that if we ignore the fundamental physical laws of science we will suffer physically. In a similar way, if we ignore the commandments of God we will also suffer. Mankind lives at the interface of the physical and the spiritual and is influenced by both the physical and the spiritual laws that God has built into the universe He has made.

God and Religion

Moving on now from the world of physical science, to look a little more carefully at how the world in which we live views the spiritual realms, we immediately see that there is an infinite number of different interpretations of what God is like. You can't look at all the world's religions without being struck by the massive discrepancies there are between them. They all believe radically different things and yet all claim to be the truth.

All the world's religions have followers who passionately, and sometimes violently, defend their version of the truth against all other versions. If only they could see that they are simply defending one version of unproven beliefs against another! It is not surprising, therefore, that in the Bible God says that He hates religion! For how can it be that all these different belief systems can be equally true? They can't.

It is remarkable that in a world where science is almost worshiped as a god, the very same people who give science such credence can then say that all religions are to be respected as if they are true! The United Nations states, for example, that:

No religion has a superior claim to truth. We all need to acknowledge and respect the pluralism of views and beliefs that exist. These values are enshrined in the founding Charter of the United Nations and if fully implemented would establish a new culture of international relations based on peace, tolerance and mutual respect. (President of the 62nd Session United Nations General Assembly, 8 October 2007)

In the world of scientific research, if there are two different understandings about something, which are at variance with each other, then all one can say is that these are two different theories under examination. For truth cannot be variable. Knowledge is knowledge, facts are facts. You cannot have two sets of supposed facts describing the same thing and say that both are true. Either one is false, or the other is false, or they are both false.

Every people group that has ever been studied by anthropologists has always had some form of worship as part of their culture. The reason for this is obvious – all of mankind is searching for a relationship with the God who made them. It is something that is built into the heart of man. So, what IS true about ALL the world's religions is that each and every one is an expression of that in-built desire to look up and worship the source of life. But what has happened in history is that each people group has made a god out of their own imagination, vested it with powers of control and then chosen to live according to those manufactured controls. They did this because they did not know the true and only God.

There are something like 3000 major religions on the face of the planet, and many more if you include variations of similar belief systems. Their followers all claim that their religion is the truth and many fear the consequences if they don't fulfill their religious duties according to the requirements of their beliefs.

If this were not such a tragic state of affairs it would be laugh-able to think that mature men and women can all believe such an extraordinary range of differing things and be willing to defend their beliefs, even to the death, because they claim to "know" that their version of the truth is true – or more true than anyone else's!

Few people have the courage to admit that if all these reli-gions are saying such different things, then they can't all be true! The only common thread of truth, that runs through all such belief systems, is that in the hearts of all men and women there is a desire for a relationship with their Creator.

God in Person!

In the absence of a relationship with God, it is impossible for mankind to deduce what God is like. We discover what people are like through relationship. The public image and the private reality of people are often very different. It is only those in close personal relationship with the individual who can be reliable wit-nesses to the person's nature and character. This brings us back to the prisoner who stood before Pontius Pilate, who declared that He had come to testify to the truth.

God knew that the only way mankind could ever gain a true understanding of His nature and character, would be if mankind could get to know Him personally and have a relationship with Him. So, God chose a people, the Jews, through whom, at a certain point in history, He would reveal Himself in human form. The whole world would then have the opportunity to know the nature and the character of God. All of mankind had been seeking this knowledge throughout history.

Of the 3000 or so world religions two are uniquely different from all the others – Judaism and Christianity. Judaism is the faith of a specific people, all of whom are descendants of Abraham,

Isaac and Jacob. These people were set apart to be the ones through whom God would reveal Himself to the whole of mankind, as the Messiah, in the form of His Son.

Christianity was birthed out of Judaism, when Messiah came. In the Scriptures the Messiah was referred to prophetically as Emmanuel, meaning *God with us*. And then He was also given the name Jesus, meaning, *for He shall save God's people from their sins.*

Jesus was the direct revelation of God to the human race. He was truth revealed. In Jesus God manifested Himself and showed His nature and character and through Jesus God made possible the restoration of relationship between Himself and His creation. Every other religion has always been founded on the back of man's attempts to find God. Christianity expresses God's plan to find man!

Christianity, therefore, is unique. No other religion can make such a claim. It is set apart from every other faith and religion by this extraordinary fact. We can be confident that Jesus Christ, the Messiah, accurately revealed God's character and nature when He lived on earth. And because Jesus, who is the embodiment of truth, affirmed the Old Testament Scriptures as the truth, we can trust that they also reveal the truth about God.

Summary

Christianity is unique. God revealed Himself to mankind so that we could know what God is like. In Jesus, we have truth revealed – the unchangeable and undeniable facts about God.

Because Jesus, who is truth, affirmed the Hebrew Scriptures as God's written Word we can, therefore, trust what the Old Testament Scriptures say about God. And because the New Testament Gospels are eye-witness accounts of the life and teaching of Jesus, the Son of God, we can trust them as further revelation about the nature and character of God.

The remainder of the New Testament was written by the early Apostolic leaders, who provided us with a remarkable eye-witness account of the early Church (the Acts of the Apostles), personal letters on how to live the life of a believer (the Epistles) and an inspired prophetic insight into the times that are yet to come (the book of Revelation). All the Scriptures as we now have them, written under the inspiration of the Holy Spirit of God, are our sourcebook for the Truth about both God and Man.

Truth Revealed

So when we put all these things together, and add to them what is written in the Bible, this is what we discover about the nature and character of God:

There is only one God, but God expresses Himself as *God the Father*, who revealed Himself to mankind through *God the Son (Jesus)* and communicates and empowers mankind through *God the Holy Spirit*. Father, Son and Holy Spirit are known as the Trinity, although the word "Trinity" is not actually found in Scripture.

God is Creator of everything that is. There is nothing in all of creation that was not created by Him or made out of things that were not created by Him. He is the Creator of all matter and He is the source of all life.

God is eternal – there is no beginning or ending to God or His Kingdom. Jesus expressed it as always being in the present – with no past and no future. He said that, *"before Abraham WAS born, I AM!"* (John 8:58, NASB, emphasis added).

God is Love. God did not decide to be loving – He IS love. If God had decided to be loving, then perhaps one day He could decide to be unloving. The nature and character of God is unchanging – yesterday, today and for ever He is the same.

God is Spirit. Jesus categorically stated that God is Spirit (John 4:24) and those who worship Him must worship Him in spirit and in truth. In saying this Jesus was indicating that we are essentially spiritual beings and that there has to be harmony between the spirit and the flesh in our worship.

God is Omnipotent. All power and all authority (the use of power) originates in Him. Jesus gave both power and authority to the disciples (Luke 9:1 – 2) so that they could go out and do the works of the Kingdom.

God is Omniscient. God knows all things. There is nothing in all creation that is outside either His knowledge or His understanding. Expressed graphically in Scripture by such statements as every hair on our head is numbered and not one sparrow falls to the ground without the Heavenly Father knowing.

God is Omnipresent. There is nowhere in all creation where we can escape from the presence of God. The Psalmist said that even if he descended to the depths of hell God would be there. There is nowhere to either hide or exist outside of His presence.

God is a God of Covenant, meaning that His promises are an outworking of who He is and that He invites us to share in everything He is. Because the nature of God is unchanging, God always keeps His covenant promises – it is man who breaks fellowship through disobedience (sin). Under the Old Covenant people were restored into relationship with God through repentance and sacrifice. In the New Covenant, there still needs to be repentance, but the ultimate sacrifice was made by God Himself when Jesus died on the cross, opening up the way for mankind to have a restored Covenant relationship with God Himself.

God, the Creator of all things, is a Father who loved the world so much that He sent His only Son to die for our sins that we might have eternal life (John 3:16).

CHAPTER 2

WHO AM I? AND WHY AM I HERE?

Having established together that God is both Creator and a God whose nature IS Love, we now need to take a hard look at ourselves. We can't think too seriously about how *to live the life* without discovering a little more about the nature of the person who is living it!

All of us had a beginning. None of us can remember it, but it is uncontestable fact that at your conception, the very moment when your father's sperm penetrated your mother's egg, there was a mini-explosion of God-ordained life and a new human being was created. YOU then began the pilgrimage of growth from fertilized egg, to a tiny embryo implanted in the lining of your mother's womb, to maturity as a baby who then made the most historic journey of your whole life and finally arrived in the world on your birthday – to then be placed in your mother's arms as you began to make an impact on your surroundings with your lungs!

While we all remember the date of our birthday, and celebrate it every year, in reality we were already nine months old when that momentous day arrived. Sometimes people make the mistake of thinking that those first nine months are just a period

35

of physical growth, but every part of our being has also been developing during this vital time of our lives – and not all the influences we have been under have necessarily been good.

We have all been influenced from conception by our generational inheritance. The Scriptures draw significant attention to people's generational lines – because they are important. Within the Ten Commandments we read that the sins of the fathers are visited upon the children until the third and the fourth generations. But it also states that the blessings go to a thousand generations of those who love the Lord and keep His commandments (Exodus 20:5–6).

Even in the Scriptures we see how the sins of one generation can have a negative effect on the succeeding generations. Just as there can be a strong genetic influence on the physical characteristics of a child – "Isn't he like his Mum (or Dad)" is probably the comment that is heard most frequently about a new arrival in the family – there can be strong spiritual influences on the personality and character of the growing child, teenager and adult.

As the years go by it is not just the physical looks which are reminders of previous generations. Behavioral and spiritual influences are just as powerfully conveyed down the generation lines. And if this is so, then there must, therefore, be a part of our creation which is fundamentally different from the physical body in which we live.

The Trinity of Man

The spirit of man: Scripture is very clear about the fact that mankind (man and woman) is more than a body. Paul prays in his letter to the Thessalonians that they might be whole in spirit, soul and body. David says in the Psalms, *"Bless the Lord, O my soul."* His spirit is speaking to his soul and telling it to worship God. And when Jesus was talking to the woman at the well He said that those who worship God must worship Him *in spirit and in truth* – implying that man must have a spirit with which to worship God and that the *"in truth"* is referring to the part of man that can make godly or ungodly (truthful or untruthful) choices.

At the beginning of Jeremiah we read these awesome words, *"Before I formed you in the womb I knew you"* (Jeremiah 1:5). This verse states, without there being any possibility of confusion, that God knew us even before we were conceived. It certainly wasn't our physical being that He could have known. Ephesians 1:4 says something similar. And perhaps most telling of all, in Genesis 1:26 God is recorded as saying, *"Let us make man in our own image, in our likeness . . ."*

The "us" is referring to the three-fold nature of the Godhead as Father, Son and Holy Spirit. So if we are made to be like God, then there will also be three dimensions to our created order – spirit, soul and body.

When people talk about Jesus, they sometimes refer to the fact that He came as a man. Scripture does the same (Philippians 2:8). The full reality of this extraordinary statement is not the incredible truth that Jesus did come to earth in the form of a man, but that originally man was created in the likeness of God. There was no other form in which Jesus could have come – He came, in appearance, as Himself and the rest of mankind looks like Him! He did not have to be transposed into what was for Him an alien creature. We were created in the first place to have an appearance like His.

Slowly we are building up a picture of the intrinsic nature of man. He is firstly a spiritual being – a spiritual being who was known by God even before our conception. In the spirit we can enjoy fellowship with God, we can communicate with Him in prayer and praise and we can know the unparalleled joy that flows from being in harmony with Him.

We can have spiritual emotions as we respond, for example, with joy or sadness to things we see happening around us as we "feel" God's point of view. We can see the beauties of God's creation and our spirit can respond by soaring in thanksgiving, as we are overwhelmed with the love, the provision and the mercy of God. In our spirit we can have God-inspired experiences, conceive visions, hear the voice of God and dream about fulfilling our destiny. And so much more as well!

The soul of man: But mankind is more than spirit, for we are tied into physical reality by our flesh. The flesh in Scripture does not refer to just the body – the flesh is the soul and the body together. For example, we read of the sins of the flesh. This does not mean that the body can sin independently of the soul. The body cannot go off and do something wrong without our agreement and instruction. The soul within us is in charge of the body and when the body is involved in something sinful, it is only doing so because the soul has made a choice to use the body for this particular purpose.

Our soul is like the driver of a machine – and our body is the machine. The two together form "the flesh." Within our soul is our mind, our emotions and our will. These three are the primary contributors to our behavior and what others may describe as our personality. With our mind we think. With our emotions we react and with our will we make decisions. And all three will motivate the soul to use our body to carry forward their thoughts and intentions into physical activity – both the good and the bad.

Just as God is able to exercise His will in a free way, one of the gifts that He gave to mankind, because we are made in His image and likeness, is that wonderful gift of free will. This is at one and the same time the most precious and yet the most dangerous thing that God gave us. Precious, because it is such an incredible privilege to use our will to make choices and be creative with all the resources we have to hand. Dangerous, because men and women have learned how to use free will to make ungodly decisions and break the covenant relationship with God. And yet, if God had not given us free will He could never have enjoyed relationship with us as we will discover below. Free will, and the capacity to enjoy relationship, go hand in hand with each other.

The body of man: Finally, there is the body, the part of our being that generally receives the most attention and yet, in the overall scheme of eternity, is the least important – only having a physical existence for a limited period of time and then waiting for resurrection as a spiritual body for eternity. And yet it is our body, from that first cry to the last breath, through which our humanity is expressed.

Our body is the most amazing of machines – a billion times more complex than any computer or machine mankind could ever construct. It is a chemical processing plant, extracting the necessary good from food and eliminating the waste. It supplies oxygen to the bodily systems via an incredibly efficient breathing machine. The oxygenated blood is pumped round the body by a heart which faithfully beats about two billion times in the average lifetime.

Our brain and our sensory organs manage and control the machine, giving constant instructions to all the muscles and bones. A thermostat controls our bodily temperature within a very narrow band of efficient operation. Our sexuality makes reproduction and the continuation of the human race possible. What an incredible machine God has given us in which to live and move and have our being on Planet Earth.

When this wonderful body is working according to the maker's instructions we say that we are well. When it is experiencing malfunction we say that we are sick. For many conditions the body acts as its own healer, fighting off infection and self-repairing such physical damage as cuts and bruises. When the conditions appear to be beyond the normal capacity of self-repair, a sick body is referred to the medical profession for treatment – we will come back later to look at the whole subject of sickness and healing.

Summary

There are three different dimensions to the being that we are. God has given us a spirit with which to relate to Him and with which to discern and enjoy spiritual things. We have a soul, which is the core of our human personality and together we live in a body which is made in the image and likeness of God. Our time on earth is limited by the life expectancy of the body. We were known by God as a spiritual being before our conception and we will continue to be known by God after our physical death. All of human life is eternal in nature. Eternal means more than lasting for ever within the framework of time – it means having an existence beyond the realms of time and beyond the existence of the physical realms.

Why Did God Make Us?

So far in this chapter we have looked at the constitution of our humanity, we now need to move on and ask the all-important questions about why God chose to make us in the first place and do we have any intrinsic value?

The good news is that God IS love – not just a God who has chosen to love us – and the word "love" only has any significance in terms of relationship. Without relationship love has no focus and no objective. Even in the Godhead there is relationship between Father, Son and Holy Spirit. On the Mount of Transfiguration Peter, James and John heard the voice of the Father from the cloud which enveloped them saying, *"This is my Son, whom I love"* (Matthew 17:5).

So both love and the expression of love are in the heart of God. It is not possible for God not to love any human being – for every human being has received life from God. Every human being is made in the image and likeness of God and every human being is loved by God. Why is it, therefore, that so many of the people who come to us for help are totally convinced that God does not love them? They can see how God must love other people, but they genuinely believe that they are the exception to God's law of love!

In most cases it is because of damage – often as a result of fathering which has not been expressive of love or, sometimes, because of the damage caused by rejection and abuse. Because others have behaved towards them in a way that is the opposite of love, they believe, deep inside, that God may not love them either. This is a major deception which we shall return to look at again in a later chapter.

So, for now, whether you have believed this in the past or not, please accept that not only is God love, *but that He also loves you.* That no matter what you have done, or what others have done to you, God's heart of love is such that He can do no other but love you and He longs for the opportunity of expressing that love towards you through relationship.

While it is possible to feel love towards someone, that the other person never knows about, it is not possible to express that love outside of a relationship. This gives us the primary key to the reason why God made you in the first place – He made you for relationship. He desires to be able to express His love towards you in relationship and He longs to hear your expression of love towards Him through that relationship also.

Being loved and feeling valued go hand in hand. A person who is loved and knows they are loved is also secure in that love, knowing that they are valued for who they are – not for what they may do. Although what we do is important, real love is independent of what we do. Your child, for example, might start being naughty at two or three years of age. Because you love your child, you don't suddenly stop loving him or her.

I was watching a film recently in which a man was about to be executed for murder. His mother knew exactly what he had done and was heart-broken because of his crime. But she still loved her son. Those last few minutes that she spent with her son, who was about to die, exposed the fact that real love transcends the barrier caused by the things people do wrong.

Where did that mother get her love from? From the God who made her. She was made in the image and likeness of God and so she was still able to love her son, even though she knew what a terrible thing he had done. None of us can say that God doesn't love us. God may, like the mother in the film, be heart-broken over what we have done and the consequences of the sins we have committed, but that doesn't stop Him loving us. *"God demonstrates his own love for us in this: While we were still sinners, Christ died for us"* (Romans 5:8).

In later chapters we will learn more about how man's relationship with God was broken in the first place and how that relationship is restored through Jesus.

Summary

There is no one that God made whom God does not love. He made us for relationship with Himself. God desires to have a relationship with every single human being and Scripture tells us in John 1:12 that "as many as receive Him" are treated by Him as His children.

CHAPTER 3

IF GOD REALLY IS GOD – WHY IS LIFE SO HARD?

This is a very good and very important question. In the answer we will discover not only why things can be so hard, but where evil comes from and why Jesus had to die. So this is a very significant chapter. It is foundational to our understanding of the world as we know it, the need for healing, the existence of so many different religions and, even, the origins of war!

The world in its original state was not the same as the world as we now know it. The early chapters of Genesis provide an encapsulated version of the story of the creation of the world and everything in it. There are key facts within the story, about which most theologians are generally in full agreement. There is also much detail missing that, with our enquiring minds, we would love to know more about. The facts that aren't there, however, do not invalidate the facts that are!

When parents, for example, are telling their first child, a three-year-old boy, that he is going to have a little brother or sister and that God has put a little baby in Mummy's tummy, they are telling the truth. It is the whole truth to the extent which a three-year-old can understand it. The many facts that are missing from this simple account of how the baby got there, do not in any way invalidate what the parents said. The fact that there is a baby in Mummy's tummy is the truth, and it is all the elder child needs to know at that stage of life.

In a similar way the Genesis account of both the creation of the universe and the early origins of mankind tell you some facts. But there are many more that are missing. And the facts that are missing in the story of creation do not in any way invalidate the facts contained in the Genesis account.

Man is constantly discovering new things about the world and the universe. I am a scientist myself, having been trained as a chemist, and I love to read about the discoveries man has made. But this does not in any way make me doubt what I read in the Word of God. I know that one day, when we are fully mature in Christ and enjoying our restored relationship with God in eternity, we will understand fully and have answers to all the impossible questions that are not obviously answered in Genesis.

We have all been tempted to ask the impossible questions that Scripture doesn't answer – such as how long was a creation day? How can we reconcile the apparent age of the universe with what Genesis seems to be saying? How was it possible for Adam and Eve's first son to find a wife for himself in the land of Nod? And so on!! For now there are many things which we have to accept by faith, without full understanding. Just as our little three-year-old grandson was content to accept "by faith" that God put a baby in Mummy's tummy, without it being necessary for him to have a full understanding of the process by which the baby got there.

What the Bible Says about Creation

So, what are the facts that we can deduce from the Genesis story which we can understand? Let's not fall into the trap of arrogance by dismissing what we can understand because there are things there that are missing from the account or some things that we don't understand! Pride is at the root of all such supposed "logic." The pride of man says that if man can't understand it, then it can't be true!

Jesus constantly affirmed the Scriptures. He never questioned their truthfulness. Even after His resurrection He expounded the Scriptures about Himself to two of His disciples on the road to Emmaus. There were things there that the disciples had not understood, but as Jesus explained them, it was as if scales were falling from their eyes, until they finally recognized who it was that was giving them such amazing revelation.

I look forward to the day when the Son of God, who made the world, takes us through the Scriptures and the scales of understanding drop from our eyes as we see the truth of the things that are there and we understand fully the things that are not immediately obvious.

Our little grandson may, one day, be a Consultant Obstetrician. His advanced knowledge of the processes of reproduction will not in any way invalidate what he was told by his parents at the age of three. God did indeed put a baby in Mummy's tummy. But there were just a few facts missing from that initial account of where babies come from that were unnecessary pieces of information at that moment in his life!

So what are the fundamental facts that we can deduce from the Genesis accounts of the history and origin of mankind, without needing to worry about the things we can't understand or which are completely missing from the story?

1. As we saw in the first chapter, God is the Creator.

2. The universe, the world and everything in it had its origin in God.

3. Everything that God had made was good, indeed very good (Genesis 1:31).

4. Mankind was a special creation. His life was God-breathed and he became *a living soul* (Genesis 2:7). These words were never used to describe the rest of creation, not even the animals.

5. Woman was created "out of man" (Genesis 2:21–24).

6. Man and woman were made in the image and the likeness of God. They had been given the gift of free will.

7. They were in fellowship and relationship with God.

8. They were given dominionship (permission to exercise authority) throughout the earth. It was to be their domain.

9. The only restriction placed upon them by their Creator was that they should not eat of the tree of the knowledge of good and evil.

   This brings us to Number 10, the key point of understanding in this chapter.

10. There was another being represented in the Garden of Eden whose motives were opposed to those of God and who had an alternative plan for mankind.

Satan's Entry onto the Stage of Planet Earth

The other being present in the Garden of Eden was Satan. The image used to illustrate him was that of a serpent. His presence is felt throughout Scripture, from Genesis to Revelation. The evidence of his activities dominates the history of mankind. Though his name is hardly ever mentioned in the media, his activities are still the focus of the news across the globe – everything from genocide to moral decay, from violence to murder, from sexual abuse to famine carries the hallmark of his work through the agency of man.

The Origin of Satan

Satan is real! Scripture tells us that he is a fallen angel who sought to elevate himself above his status as an archangel. His original name was probably Lucifer, bringer of light, and as such he was a splendid and very beautiful creation of God. Most commentators interpret Isaiah 14:12–15 as describing how Satan (Lucifer – portrayed as the king of Babylonia) vowed to make himself "like the Most High." As a result there was rebellion in the heavenly realms, and there was no way in which this angel, who had chosen to use his free will to oppose his Creator, could be allowed to remain.

Revelation 12 describes the ensuing war in heaven when Michael, the archangel and chief warrior angel, was sent with his warrior forces to do battle with Lucifer and his angels. *"And the great dragon was thrown down, the serpent of old who is called the devil and Satan, who deceives the whole world; he was thrown down to the earth, and his angels were thrown down with him"* (Revelation 12:9, NASB).

From then on Lucifer was no longer called Lucifer, meaning "light," but Satan, meaning "adversary" or one who is hostile to and opposes God. In Luke 10, Jesus adds His own personal account of how Satan was thrown out of heaven. He was talking to the seventy-two who returned full of joy, because they had found the demons actually obeyed their commands.

It was important that Jesus should put their exuberance into context and remind them that He had all power and authority in the first place. He was there when Satan was expelled from heaven and He had the authority to delegate His power and authority to those whom He chose.

Satan, with all his angels, was thrown down to earth. As an archangel he had been a very powerful spiritual being, but on Planet Earth he had no spiritual authority. This meant that he had no means of receiving worship from those who obeyed him – receiving worship for himself had been the desire of his heart. It was this that had led to his downfall. Power cannot be exercised without authority. A boxer has power in his muscles and fists, but he only has authority to use that power in a boxing ring. Outside the ring his power is unusable. Satan was a bit like a boxer without a ring in which to fight. He had power but no authority.

What Happened in the Garden

Man as he is now, is not as he was first created. God is holy and righteous, and He made man in His own image. So somewhere, at some time, something must have gone sadly wrong. However one interprets the story of Adam, Eve, the Garden of Eden and the serpent, the consequences of the Fall are exactly as Genesis relates. The evidence all around us does not contradict the simple conclusion of the Genesis story. Man has become a creature of sin and his behavior is a constant reminder that he is in rebellion against a holy and righteous God.

As soon as we mention the word *rebellion*, we are reminded of what happened in the heavenly realms when Lucifer tried to take for himself the glory that belonged to God. Rebellion in the heavenly ranks could not be tolerated and Lucifer was expelled and thrown down to earth. Rebelliousness had become part of Satan's character.

Having been frustrated in his first endeavor to dethrone God Himself, Satan set about destroying what God had made. He targeted man, the pinnacle of God's creation, made in the image and likeness of God Himself, and his primary tactic was to sow the seeds of rebellion, to infect mankind with his own spirit.

Rebellion is like a contagious disease for which there is no cure – once caught, you have it for life. The essence of all sin is rebellion, and the heart of the Genesis account of the Fall of man is simply that – rebellion against the instructions that God had given.

The greatest but most risky gift that God gave to man was his free will. At no time has God ever overridden this capacity for us to choose to do our own thing. Adam and Eve had free will to choose. As long as there were no seeds of rebellion sown in their hearts, the concept of choosing anything but obedience to God's loving direction would never have entered their heads. Up to that point they had used their free will wisely. To eat of the tree of the knowledge of good and evil was not a thought they could have entertained.

In the Genesis story Satan is portrayed as a serpent, a picture that is consistent with Jesus' comment to the seventy-two – "*I have given you authority to trample on snakes and scorpions and to overcome all the power of the enemy; nothing will harm you*" (Luke 10:19). Here, Jesus was making a statement about the authority that believers in Him can have over Satan and all the works of the enemy.

The subtlety of Satan was to encourage Eve to doubt what God had said and not to believe that the consequences of eating such luscious fruit could possibly end in death. At this point Eve had not sinned, but she was contemplating an act of rebellion. The moment she took of the fruit, rebellion was no longer a thought in her head but an action that had been carried out with her whole being.

Sin had entered the human race and the rebellion that began with Satan in heaven had now contaminated mankind. Adam followed Eve's example, and the disease of sin became endemic for the whole of the human race. Man had fallen from his primary, sinless, state.

God had planned that man, who is primarily a spiritual being, should always live in total harmony and fellowship with Him.

There is nothing in the Scripture to indicate whether that was to have been eternal life on earth or in heaven. Just as Satan couldn't continue in fellowship with God and had to be expelled from heaven, it is clear that the human race couldn't remain in close fellowship with God in that special Garden. Adam and Eve had joined in Satan's rebellion against God.

God's prophetic word to Eden's first and only gardeners became true: *"you must not eat from the tree of the knowledge of good and evil, for when you eat of it you will surely die"* (Genesis 2:17). When they did eat of this tree the intimate spiritual relationship, which man had formerly enjoyed with God, died also. Death had entered into the human race. Spiritual death was handed down to the soul and physical death became the inheritance of the body on Planet Earth. And physical death is something that no sinful human being has ever been able to avoid!

The Consequences of the Fall

God had chosen to sentence Satan and all his angels to immediate expulsion from heaven and subsequent eternal punishment in the lake of fire (Revelation 20:7–15; Matthew 25:41–46). Having once dealt with rebellion so justly, firmly and finally, there was no way that God could not deal firmly with similar rebellion in man. As Paul says in Romans 6:23, *"the wages of sin is death,"* and as, through Adam and Eve, sin entered the world, so also was the judgment of God brought upon the world. By joining in with Satan's rebellion against God, they also contracted to share in the judgment that had been meted out to Satan. That may sound hard, but it is fair.

I sometimes teach this as mankind choosing to get on board Satan's bus! It's as if Satan is driving a bus, on the front of which is a destination board saying "Hell." When Adam and Eve chose to climb aboard, they were not anticipating that, without the intervention of Jesus, hell would be their destination. But they suddenly discovered they were trapped as passengers on a bus who would one day end up at the same destination as the driver. God did not choose to send man to hell, but man chose to join Satan and, therefore, could not avoid participating in Satan's judgment and destination.

God's heart must have broken when He saw what human beings had chosen to do with the free will they had been entrusted with. In most legal jurisdictions, an accessory to a crime is as guilty as the man who commits the crime. Adam and Eve may only have been accessories to Satan's "crime," but they, and all after them, were, and still are, guilty of complicity!

Why is Life So Hard?

So let's go back now to the question in the title of this chapter, which we are now better equipped to answer. Why is life so hard?

Man was originally given dominionship over the Earth – that means permission to exercise authority and have absolute freedom to live in, enjoy, benefit from and control the whole planet. Quite a commission! But it is a fact that if you are under someone else's authority, whatever authority you do have is controlled by the one you obey. That person can take advantage of and use whatever authority you have. So, when mankind chose to obey Satan by eating of the tree of the knowledge of good and evil, not only did death enter into the human race, as the relationship with God was broken, but mankind's dominionship (his authority) then became subject to Satan's control.

In one devastatingly successful maneuver Satan had not only gained control of the planet, but he had also engineered things so that mankind now worshiped him. In all religions, obedience is an expression of worship, so the first expression of religion was established on Planet Earth, when mankind followed and obeyed Satan's voice. Satan is a spiritual being. He is masquerading as if he is God and rejoices to receive worship through everything mankind does which is in rebellion against the living God, the God of covenant love. Paul called him *"the god of this world"* (2 Corinthians 4:4, NASB) and John said the whole world is under his control (1 John 5:19).

The effect on the human race was immediate. Adam and Eve were expelled from the Garden, where everything had been provided for them. Child-bearing would now become a difficult and painful experience for women, and the ground was now cursed and as a result the growing of crops for food would become hard work. There would be opposition from the very ground in the form of weeds (thorns and thistles). Everything would become tough. And not only would life be hard, but it would also be cut short – in all sorts of ways, through sickness and disease, through murder, war and accident. The price of rebellion was, and always has been, very high.

Summary

Life is tough because we have an enemy of souls who was handed authority over the planet by mankind. Man has only ever been able to move forward by overcoming the opposition of his sworn enemy. Satan opposes everything that comes from God – even the birth of new God-given life – and as soon as we turn our face towards obedience of God we come up against the opposition of the god of this world. All the bad things that happen in the world are a direct consequence of Satan's activity. While none of us can escape the consequences of living in a fallen world, there is another chapter in the story!

CHAPTER 4

GOD'S RESCUE PLAN FOR THE HUMAN RACE

Because God is love, even when mankind rebelled against Him it did not change His heart of love towards human beings. Just as a parent should not cease to love his or her child when they do something wrong, so God did not cease to love the human race, or any individual human being, when they, mankind, chose to go Satan's way. God's love for every single human being is unshakeable and is not related in any way to our behavior, whether it is sinful or godly! He loves us because we ARE, not because of what we do or don't do.

That does not mean to say that there aren't consequences for sin – there are. Sin separated the human race from the intimacy of relationship with God in the first place and our ongoing sins continue to cause grief to the heart of God. The personal pain of grief is only experienced because of love. No love – no grief! You don't feel personal pain when something goes wrong in another person's life, unless you have love for that person and are, therefore, affected by what has happened. God is always affected by the sins of mankind.

But the personal pain of grief also motivates the heart. We are all motivated to do something for someone we love when something bad happens in their life. Where do those feelings come from? From God, for we are made in His image and likeness and respond in ways that are similar to the ways He responds. When we want to stretch out our hand and rescue someone we love, it is a direct reflection of what God decided to do when man chose to follow Satan. God stretched out more than His hand, He planned to give of His very best.

The Prophecies of Scripture

The first prophetic word of Scripture warned of what would happen if Adam and Eve ate of the tree of the knowledge of good and evil. The second prophetic word was directly from God to Satan, in which He said that, one day, the offspring of woman would crush Satan's head! (Genesis 3:15). The head always refers to authority, so if the head is crushed, it means that there is going to be an offspring of woman who will not be under Satan's control, but will have a higher authority. This is the first place in Scripture where we read of the promised Messiah – the one who would rescue all of us from the enemy of souls.

There are a multitude of similar promises throughout the Old Testament. The consistency of the prophetic message, from one generation of prophetic people to the next, is awesome in its impact. There is hardly a book in the Bible which does not make reference to the coming Messiah – the anointed one of God who would come from God to rescue mankind.

As part of the strategy and plan, God chose a man, Abraham, and set him apart to be the father of a new nation. A nation to whom God gave a land, but to whom He also gave an identity. The hallmark of God has always been upon the Jewish people, even to this day. No other nation of people has suffered such attacks – just because of who they are. They have survived close on 100 attempts at genocide. Six million were slaughtered by Hitler alone, just because they were Jews.

But even though the Jewish people have been scattered to every country of the world, they have maintained their unique identity as Jewish people. Throughout history the Jews have been high achievers, at the very forefront of the arts, the sciences and of literature. The number of Jews that have been awarded Nobel Prizes is way out of proportion relative to the number of Jews there are in the world, when compared with the people in all the other nations. The genius of God, the creativity of the Creator, is uniquely upon this most persecuted of peoples.

Why should such an extraordinarily successful group of people be so hated? The only reason is that the god of this world hates the people through whom Messiah came and he stirs up enmity against them. Satan also knows that once the Jews come to recognize Yeshua (Jesus) as their Messiah, his days of power will soon be over and the second coming of the Messiah will be at hand.

It was the prophet Isaiah who saw this Messianic figure dying on behalf of others. Writing in the prophetic past, as if this future event had already taken place, he said, *"he was pierced for our transgressions, he was crushed for our iniquities; the punishment that brought us peace was upon him, and by his wounds, we are healed"* (Isaiah 53:5).

Throughout their history, in response to the instructions God had given them through Moses, the Jews were used to dealing with their sins through repentance and sacrifice – usually the sacrifice of animals and birds. But the sacrifice of a human being was something very different. Why would such a sacrifice be necessary? Wouldn't the animal sacrifices be enough?

It was through the sacrificial system that sins could be forgiven, but there is an important difference between the forgiveness of sins and the restoration of relationship with Father

God. The Psalmist says, *"Blessed is he whose transgressions are forgiven, whose sins are covered. Blessed is the man whose sin the Lord does not count against him"* (Psalm 32:1).

In Old Testament times people could be forgiven for their sins, but still not be able to enter into the sort of relationship with God that Adam had before the Fall. People could live in obedience to God, obey the commandments of God (Exodus 20:1–17), fulfill the conditions of Covenant (Deuteronomy 28:1–14) and be very blessed by God in this fallen world. But the god of this world would still be there, exercising spiritual authority on earth and separating mankind in time from the possibility of enjoying fellowship with God in heaven in eternity.

So, even the greatest saints of the Old Testament, many of whose names are to be found in Hebrews 11, died with their sins forgiven, but still separated by the curse of death from the God they loved and the God who loved them. Hebrews 11:39 puts it this way, *"none of them received what had been promised."* They had received forgiveness, but the Messianic promises were for even more than forgiveness, they were for the removal of all the barriers between man and God so that full relationship could be restored, unimpeded by anything of the sinful nature that is common to all humanity.

But in another prophecy Isaiah saw something else. Talking of what the Messiah would do when He came, he said, *"The Spirit of the Sovereign Lord is on me, because the Lord has anointed me to preach good news to the poor. He has sent me to bind up the broken-hearted, to proclaim freedom for the captives and release from darkness for the prisoners"* (Isaiah 61:1).

And this prophecy is different from the promises of forgiveness: this speaks of restoration – both the restoration of healing and the restoration of relationship with Father God. It speaks of prisoners being set free.

Who are the prisoners? It certainly doesn't mean people in jail, although the Jews of Jesus' day were looking for a Messianic figure who would set them free from the control of Rome! No, the prisoners are everyone who is under Satan's control. So this promise is a confirmation of Genesis 3:15, that when Messiah comes He is going to deal with the authority of Satan – the authority that was given to him by man – so that the captives may be set free from Satan's control and be free again to relate with Father God. No longer will the curse of death be able to keep mankind, God's special creation, from enjoying fellowship with God.

But How Can This Happen?

Man had been given free will by God, and then he had been given authority over the world. But then he used that free will to hand control of the world into Satan's hands. God could not go against the free-will choice that man had made. The only way that the human race could find a way of escape, would be if a man could be found to be a representative of the people, who had not been tainted by the sinful decision that gave Satan control and had not, therefore, come under Satan's control. But where could a sinless man be found, when every human being had been conceived under the regime of sin that prevailed in the world?

In the Old Testament the special name given to the Messiah is Emmanuel, meaning "God with us" (Isaiah 7:14). This is a direct reference to the fact that if God was going to rescue us from Satan's control, He would have to take action Himself. No one under Satan's control could ever deal with Satan's authority. You would need to have a higher, or greater authority.

When, at last, it was the time for Jesus to come, the Jewish people were under the domination of a Roman occupying power, and the only Messiah most of the people were looking for was someone who would rid them of this tyranny. The majority of the leaders in that day were blinded to what the Scriptures really said. Only a handful of people were actually ready and alert in their spirit to welcome Jesus into the world.

Joseph and Mary had been warned by angelic visitations. They must have been totally dazed by the enormity of what was happening to them. When Gabriel said that Mary would conceive a child by the Holy Ghost, the implication of these words is that the child would be unlike any other. He would not be conceived through sexual relationships, thus carrying the taint of sin further down the generation lines. The child would be born sinless, a second Adam – the last Adam, as Paul would later refer to Him (1 Corinthians 15:45).

This child would not inherit the curse of death and would not be separated from Father God by the spiritual authority of Satan. He would inherit the mantle of spiritual authority, implicit in the word "dominionship." He would be able to say with absolute truth that *"All authority has been given unto me"* (Matthew 28:18). His authority was indeed higher than Satan's. No wonder Satan did everything he could to destroy this child, even to the extent of encouraging Herod to kill all the babies in Bethlehem. This baby was a real threat to Satan's world domination.

How encouraged Joseph and Mary must have been when they took the baby Jesus up to the Temple to find two very elderly people, Simeon and Anna, who knew exactly who this baby was and whose lives were totally fulfilled by that brief encounter with Messianic destiny. While visits from angels are very special, the assurance and encouragement of human beings is also very, very precious.

How Joseph and Mary must have rejoiced when Simeon came out with those beautiful words, which have been the inspiration for songs of worship in every era of the Church and all over the world, *"Lord, now lettest thou thy servant depart in peace, according to thy word; for mine eyes have seen thy salvation which thou hast prepared in the presence of all peoples, a light for revelation to the Gentiles, and for glory to thy people Israel"* (Luke 2:29–32, RSV).

Simeon knew then that he could die in peace. The child that God had told him about had finally been born. He had delivered his word of affirmation and encouragement to the parents – and to the world. His life's work – just a few minutes of eternally precious time – was over. God had indeed fulfilled His word. And at that very same hour, along came the second prophetic witness, Anna, eighty-four years of age, but still fasting and praying and never ceasing to worship God. What a lady! And how precious of the Lord to send both a man and a woman to testify to Joseph and Mary – two witnesses, each affirming the other's testimony as to the identity of the baby in their arms.

Joseph had been told by the angel to call the baby "Jesus," His New Testament (New Covenant) name, for He would *"save His people from their sins"* (Matthew 1:21, NASB). But Mary and Joseph were told nothing of how Jesus would achieve this objective. As Jews they would have known about the promise of a coming Messiah, but it is unlikely that they would have understood that their son would die a cruel death for the sins of the world.

Why Did Jesus Have to Die?

Jesus stated the facts of the matter quite simply, in His conversation with Nicodemus, that *"God so loved the world [the people He had created] that he gave his one and only Son, that whoever believes in him shall not perish but have eternal life"* (John 3:16). That Scripture is perhaps the most-quoted and best-loved verse in the whole Bible.

The implication of these words, however, is not free pardon for all, come what may, but free pardon for those who believe. If a person chooses not to believe, the result is inevitable – a share, with Satan, in the consequences of rebellion, which, according to Matthew, Hebrews and Revelation, means the lake of fire and the second death!

It was as soon as man first sinned, at the very moment when time began to run out for the human race, that God put into effect His plan for a way of escape. He chose to send His Son to earth to live and die as a human being but to remain without sin. As such, Jesus could take upon Himself the punishment for our sin – but should He sin, the plan would fail. For it was only by not joining in Satan's rebellion that the way would be open for those who are trusting Jesus to be saved from the consequences of their own rebellion.

For Jesus, the temptations in the wilderness were very real. Satan was desperate to divert Jesus from His divine mission. Had Jesus chosen to use His divine powers for selfish ends His mission would have failed. He could have made bread for Himself when He was hungry at a time when He was fasting, or accepted Satan's offer of all the kingdoms of the world without going to the cross. He could have jumped off the pinnacle of the Temple to impress people with the aerial expertise of the angels in protecting Him from harm, or succumbed to any other temptation that Satan threw at Him. If He had given in to Satan, and done what Satan was asking of Him, even the Son of God would have been seen to be no better than mankind in coping with the attacks of the enemy and Jesus would have come under Satan's authority and control.

Because Jesus was sinless, death was not His rightful inheritance. If He physically died, death would have no authority to hold Him in the grave. The sinless Son of God was the only possible threat to Satan's rule. Several times Satan tried to kill Jesus prematurely. But it was only when the time on God's prophetic calendar finally arrived, and Jesus voluntarily chose to lay down His life, that He finally faced death. And Satan knew that Jesus was about to overcome him.

For Jesus to die willingly, and at the appointed time, meant that God was opening up a way for countless millions of people to be released from Satan's jail and be restored to God the Father. God is a just God – and the price for sin had to be paid. And here was One who was not subject to death offering Himself as the sacrifice. No wonder John the Baptist said of Jesus, *"Behold, the Lamb of God who takes away the sin of the world"* (John 1:29, NASB).

Jesus was the sacrificial lamb, not just for the Jewish people, but for the whole world. He chose to lay down His life, and therein lies the heart of the story of the cross and resurrection. Because He was not subject to death, He could pay the price of death and carry upon His shoulders the sins of the whole world, without death being His permanent condition! God planned that the price of sin would be paid, by the only one who could pay the price, and live to triumph over the grave – Himself!

And so, thirty-six hours after His terrible suffering and death, on the day we call Good Friday, an angel rolled away the stone and Jesus burst forth from the grave. Not only had Jesus been the sacrificial lamb, but He had conquered death and the greatest consequence of the Fall had been overcome. Jesus had personally vanquished Satan, death had not been able to hold Him.

All Satan's demons were placed firmly under the feet of Jesus Christ, and the greatest victory in the history of the world had been staged, played out and proclaimed. The price had been paid and salvation had been won for all those who are willing to receive the glorious good news for themselves, accept the Savior and make Him Lord of their lives. What a glorious inheritance for those who believe and receive!

Jesus came to earth, or as John so graphically expressed it, *"the Word became flesh, and dwelt among us"* (John 1:14, NASB). He came as a man but remained totally sinless. He resisted all temptations and never came under Satan's control. He conquered death. He ascended to glory and now sits at the right hand of the Father, having achieved everything the Father had asked of Him. And the highway that was opened up by Jesus is one that you and I can walk on. It is a highway of holiness – not our holiness, but His. Not only can our sins now be forgiven, but there can also be a restoration of relationship with Father God.

The way was opened for people to be able to enter heaven on this highway of holiness and the offer has been open ever since, to all who would come and be born again into a new, restored and eternal relationship with God: *"as many as received Him, to them He gave the right to become children of God"* (John 1:12, NASB).

No wonder Jesus underlined in His ministry that He was the only way to the Father (John 14:1–7). It was only a sinless man that could pay the price and open up the way of salvation. There was and is no other way. Jesus is *"the way and the truth and the life"* (John 14:6). The rescue plan was complete. On the cross Jesus defeated Satan and gave us the opportunity of being freed from all the curses that mankind had suffered because of the Fall. Jesus *"became a curse for us"* (Galatians 3:13, RSV) that we might live!

Summary

The Fall was real and has resulted in man's separation from God through rebellion. God's love is such that He sent Jesus to open up a way for the relationship between God and man to be restored. That way is open for all who believe in Jesus.

As we repent of our own sinfulness, and receive Him as our Savior, a two-way transaction takes place. We enter into Him and He enters into us. We receive new life – often expressed as being born again. As part of Him we have, therefore, the benefit of sharing in everything that He has been through – including His death upon the cross. In Him we have already died.

The consequences of our sin have been borne by Him and not only have we died, but in Him we have also been raised again from the dead and are alive for evermore. Our physical death, when it comes is no longer to be feared – it no longer has any sting for the believer (1 Corinthians 15:55) for we have already died, been raised from the dead and are alive for evermore!

Jesus' relationship with Father God was never broken. Therefore, because I am in Him, my relationship with Father God is restored. I am alive in Him for eternity!

The essence of the gospel is incredibly simple. The way is open for all who choose to accept the salvation Jesus won for us, to enter into the Kingdom of God by being born again of the Spirit of God. Our first birth was into a world which is overshadowed by death – our second birth is into a relationship, with Jesus, made possible through resurrection life. There are no restrictions and it is totally free – it is indeed a gospel for all – even for the poor!

Beginning the Journey of Life – the Sinner's Prayer

If you have never really understood the message of the gospel before and you now want to become a Christian and be born again, I suggest you read carefully through the following prayer and then pray it again, out loud, as you accept by faith forgiveness for all your sins and are born again as a child of God.

A Prayer of Salvation

Thank You, Jesus, for dying on the cross for me. I confess that I am a sinner in need of a Savior. I ask You to come into my life now, to forgive me for all my sin and to cleanse me from all unrighteousness. I invite You to come and reign in my life and be Lord of every area of my being. Thank You, Lord, for my new birth, my new life and my new destiny. I choose to live for You all my days. Amen.

You may only have been a Christian for a very short time, or you may have been a believer for many years. However long ago it is since you were born again, you have taken that tremendous *step from death to LIFE* – a life which you can enjoy now and which will continue beyond the grave.

God's Deposit in Your Life!

When you became a Christian you were born again of the Spirit of God. Paul expressed one aspect of this amazing truth in this way in Ephesians 1:13–14:

> *Having believed, you were marked in him with a seal, the prom-*
> *ised Holy Spirit, who is a deposit guaranteeing our inheritance*
> *until the redemption of those who are God's possession – to the*
> *praise of his glory.*

God placed a deposit of the Holy Spirit within you. A deposit is a down-payment in anticipation of full ownership.

I once put a deposit down on a car I wanted to buy. I knew it was mine, even though I hadn't yet taken full possession of it. It was a bit like that when you became a Christian – you belonged to God from the moment that Holy Spirit deposit was placed within you. But it is only when we finally enter into heaven's glory that all the shackles of sin will be shaken away and we will receive our full inheritance. For now we have a deposit – but then we will know full redemption.

For now we have a life to live! It is true that one day you will die and make that amazing transition into eternity with God, and we must all be ready for that moment whenever it comes, but all of us are expecting that a few years will pass before we are called home. Right now, therefore, we need to know how to live here on earth as we continue with our earthly pilgrimage and that's what the rest of this book is all about.

CHAPTER 5

BECOMING A DISCIPLE OF THE KING

The Race of Life

Just for a moment use your imagination! Imagine that you have just become a Christian. Imagine that you are now ready to really start living!

It's as if you are standing there at the beginning of a race. You don't know when or where the end of the race will come, but you do know where you are right now. Jesus is Lord of your life. Your sins are forgiven. You have a new relationship with Father God. This is the first day of the rest of your life and a whole world of opportunity is stretching out before you. You can sense that life with a capital L is just about to start. The starter has fired his gun and you are off!

All is well in those heady early moments of the race of life as you set off with much enthusiasm. But it isn't long before you are beginning to feel the pace and you begin to experience opposition. You thought your desire and intention to serve the Lord would be unwavering, but it seems as though it is being challenged and you are not sure where the opposition is coming from.

As a young believer you are struggling with trying to understand why you feel the way you do.

Instead of feeling the freedom of the open road ahead, with the wind of joy blowing you gently along, the gentle breeze that was behind you has become a cold wind of opposition that cuts right through you. And from behind you are feeling tugs of resistance, as if there are forces trying to pull you back and slow you down. Is this really what the Christian life is supposed to be like? Questioning voices begin to challenge your commitment and you may even wonder if you are on the right road.

The Park of Good Intentions

Then just ahead, by the side of the road, you see a stretch of gentle parkland. It looks very attractive and welcoming. Some are stopping here – accepting an invitation to come and rest, being told that they can get up and carry on running whenever they feel like it.

The seats in the parkland look very comfortable. But then you realize that the people on the seats look as though they've been there for a very long time. And there don't seem to be any people getting up from their seats and carrying on with the race. Suddenly you realize that while there is a way into the park, there doesn't seem to be a way out.

Just in time you realize it's a trap, designed to take you off the road, never to return. Cold sweat begins to break out on your brow as you realize how close you were to dropping out of the race. You press on past those that are encouraging you to stop for a rest. It is only then that you are able to see a sign which says, *"You have now passed the Park of Good Intentions."*

Of course, this is just a story, but it does illustrate that many people set off to live the Christian life with enthusiasm, but very quickly get sidelined by the pressures of life and opposition from the enemy of souls. Jesus taught something similar when He said that there are four types of ground on which the seed of the Kingdom can fall, the hard ground, the stony ground, the ground where there is a lot of competition from thorns and thistles and finally the good ground (Matthew 13:1–23).

The good news of the gospel is very attractive. Deep in most people's hearts there is a realization that they need to be forgiven. And when the offer of salvation is made they respond gladly, knowing that their destination needs to change. But if the offer of salvation is made solely on the basis of it being an escape route from the wrong destination when you die, and there is little or no teaching about salvation being a choice between living, here on earth, under the authority of the god of this world or entering a new kingdom and choosing to live under the authority of a new King, it is easy to give up and go back.

It's no wonder that many do not understand what they have really done in becoming a Christian and choose to rest in the *Park of Good Intentions*. Depending on the belief that they are now "born again," they carry on living as they always did, with little change in life-style, thinking that their "born again" ticket will still be valid when they pass through the gates which divide this life from the next!

Sadly, in the parable Jesus told, the birds of the air came and ate the seed that fell on hard ground – implying that those who didn't understand the message about the Kingdom would fall away because the birds of the air had consumed the seed. These birds of the air represent the evil one who snatches away what was sown in their hearts (Matthew 13:19).

Those who understand the message about the Kingdom, know that they are now living under the authority of a new King. The gift of discernment will help them to recognize attacks from the enemy and take avoiding or remedial action. Even though their ground may be stony, and in danger of being over-run by

weeds, they want to press on, clean up their patch and increase
in fruitfulness. Much of this book is about how to rid the ground
of stones and weed the patch, so that the ground becomes good
and productive.

In another parable Jesus talks about our lives in the context
of a vine in a vineyard. God desires and intends that our lives
should bear much fruit, but to make the vine fruitful, there has
to be some serious pruning. The branches that remain can then
produce the maximum amount of fruit.

Both pictures are relevant to living the Christian life. Sometimes we have to remove the stones from the ground ourselves,
at other times we must allow the Father (who is the gardener)
to prune our branches. The end result in both cases is greater
fruitfulness for the Kingdom and greater joy in our relationship
with God, as we enter into our destiny as God's Kingdom people.

What If?

I love reading Christian biography – especially the detailed personal stories of the great pioneers of the faith who did great
things and achieved much in the Kingdom of God. I like to read
of people like John Wesley, the extraordinary eighteenth-century
evangelist, and William Carey, the father of the modern missionary movement, who translated the Bible into all the major Indian
languages.

I thrill to the story of Hudson Taylor, the man who, more
than any other, was responsible for opening up China to the gospel, and Gladys Aylward who, in later years, followed in Hudson
Taylor's footsteps. Then there are the stories of D.L. Moody and
Billy Graham, the most famous of America's great evangelists,
and Jackie Pullinger, the "angel" of Hong Kong who learned
within the old walled city how to live in the gifts and fruit of the
Holy Spirit and set drug captives free. I could go on and on, there

are hundreds of such people, whose dynamic stories are both inspiring and instructive.

Their stories inspire believers to trust the God who has called them to Himself and to believe for what seems impossible. They instruct us in the ways of God as we discover how these amazing men and women of God chose to be more than believers and become disciples. They didn't just come to Jesus, claim their salvation and spend the rest of their days serving themselves whilst waiting to enter heaven after they had died! They literally took hold of that for which Christ Jesus had taken hold of them (Philippians 3:12) and changed for ever the particular part of the world into which God had sent them.

Thousands of missionaries were inspired by Hudson Taylor and followed in his steps. To this day I wear a prayer covenant ring that was given to one of these missionaries, who served under Hudson Taylor in China, having been called to the task through attending a prayer meeting started by my great-uncle and my grandfather for Hudson Taylor's China Inland Mission.

When I first went to India my host stood at the airport with his open Telegu Bible. With a beaming smile on his face he said to me (an Englishman), *"Thank you for sending Carey!"* It was William Carey who had translated the Scriptures into Telegu, enabling him, several generations later, to come to know Jesus and find faith in God.

What if these few had stayed at home? What if they had listened to the voices of doubters and antagonists who tried to convince them that the particular call of God upon their life wasn't for them? William Carey, for example, had to endure ten years of such opposition from his own church fellowship! What if he and others had rested in the *Park of Good Intentions?*

The *What if?* scenario doesn't bear thinking about. Countless millions of people would not have come to know the truth about Jesus and would not now be in the Kingdom of God. For example, the amazing move of God in the underground Church in mainland China, in the years since the communists took over that great land, would not have happened.

The call to discipleship is at the heart of what it means to live the life of a Christian. What adventures, what privileges, what fulfillment awaits those who choose to be wholly available to God as a faithful disciple of Jesus Christ and a citizen of the Kingdom of God.

Citizens of the Kingdom

Becoming a Christian is far, far more than just believing that Jesus is Lord. As James so aptly puts it in his letter: *"Even the demons believe that – and shudder"* (James 2:19). So, if believing in God is something that even the demons can do, there has to be something much deeper and more significant associated with truly following Jesus and living life God's way!

After the resurrection Jesus spent many days talking with the disciples, teaching them and *"giving instructions through the Holy Spirit to the apostles he had chosen...He appeared to them over a period of forty days **and spoke about the Kingdom of God**"* (Acts 1:2–3, emphasis added).

These were very precious days – unforgettable days for the Apostles. They had gone from disaster (on Good Friday) to triumph (on resurrection morning). What a roller-coaster of a journey! The man they had followed for three years had indeed fulfilled His destiny and shortly He was going to return to heaven's glory. They knew His time with them was limited and they would have been hanging onto His every word.

I'm sure that during these forty days the Gospel writers would have been making notes, as Jesus reminded them of one thing after another that He'd taught them, and the events

Becoming A Disciple Of The King   71

they had experienced together, during the three years of His ministry.

It seems that the main thrust of what Jesus was teaching them was not about how to preach the gospel, so that people would be born again of the Spirit of God, important though that was, but about what it really means to be living as citizens of the Kingdom of God. It was knowledge of the Kingdom which Jesus considered critical to the body of believers who would lead the New Testament Church. Without this knowledge believers would be unlikely to become disciples.

The Great Commission

Just before Jesus ascended to heaven, Matthew recorded the last earthly words that Jesus said. Then He left His disciples to get on with the job of building the Church. These last words of Jesus are usually referred to as the Great Commission. It is these words which most Christian denominations take as their mandate for evangelism, given by Jesus Himself to the whole of the Church for the whole of time! It is these words that need to occupy our attention as we consider how to live the life that Father God has given back to us, through Jesus.

> *"All authority in heaven and on earth has been given to me.*
> *Therefore go and make disciples of all nations, baptising them*
> *in the name of the Father and of the Son and of the Holy Spirit,*
> *and teaching them to obey everything I have commanded you.*
> *And surely I am with you always, to the very end of the age."*
> (Matthew 28:18–20)

Let's first look at what this commission doesn't say – it doesn't say go and make believers. Does that mean that the disciples weren't believers? Not at all. But it does mean that Jesus doesn't seem to recognize here the possibility of believers who wouldn't also become disciples! And for many that is quite a radical thought.

So what does it say? It begins by affirming that Jesus has all authority in His hand. This means that whatever authority Satan as the god of this world has, Jesus has a higher authority. Those who are serving Jesus also have a higher authority, delegated to them by Jesus, and this enables them to live for and serve the Lord, even in the alien environment of a world that is hostile to the truth about Jesus.

It was through this delegated authority that the disciples had been able to go and proclaim the Kingdom, heal the sick and cast out demons, during the time that they were followers of Jesus, in the early days of His ministry (Luke 9:1–2).

The Great Commission instructed those first disciples to go to all nations – that means all people groups – not just countries. In some countries there are many different people groups. Their commission is to make more disciples – so what does that mean for us who, many generations of believers down the line from the Apostles, are wanting to live the life that we have been called to?

In general terms a disciple is someone who does the things that the teacher has taught. But in more specific terms, in respect of the disciples of Jesus, they were known as people who had left everything to follow Jesus and were now committed to be the pioneer leaders of the Body of believers. They were to be citizens of heaven (living under the authority of the King of Heaven) at the same time as proclaiming the truth about the King here on earth.

So, in becoming a believer in Jesus, you now have a choice to make. Are you going to be a believer in Jesus whose belief does not really make any difference to the way you live? Or are you going to be a believer who presses on in the faith, intent on being what Jesus has called you to be – a disciple of the King and a citizen of the Kingdom of God? If so, please read on!

A Disciple of the King

I am assuming you've chosen to live as a disciple of the King. What does that mean? The Apostle Paul often uses military terminology to describe aspects of the Christian life. To continue with Paul's style of military illustration, all military personnel, of whatever nation and whichever branch of the armed forces they are serving in, operate under standing orders.

The standing orders are those basic instructions and conduct of behavior which are expected of all military personnel at all times. For example, you don't need to be told to salute a senior officer, you just do it. There are many such standing orders. A consequence of obedience to standing orders is that all members of the armed forces are ready for action at any time. Fulfilling one set of instructions equips them for being obedient to specific orders they may be given at any time.

Living the Christian life can be looked at in a similar way – there are the standing orders and the specific instructions. The standing orders include everything from prayer and reading the Bible to meeting in fellowship with other believers for worship and teaching. The standing orders include living according to scriptural standards of morality and with godly integrity. Your lips speak truth and you can be trusted to be a man of your word. Your heart's desire is to serve the Lord, not just behave as if you are serving the Lord, while on the inside there's rebellion!

All these basic standing orders can be summed up in an instruction that Paul gave to Timothy, a young leader in training, when he said, *"Watch your life and doctrine closely. Persevere in them, because if you do, you will save both yourself and your hearers"* (1 Timothy 4:16).

Earlier in the chapter Paul had spelled out to Timothy how important his speech, life, love, faith and purity were (verse 12) and in verse 8 Paul had said, *"physical training is of some value, but godliness has value for all things, holding promise for both the present life and the life to come."* A godly life is at the heart of the standing orders of a disciple of Jesus.

Worship is more than singing! A more Hebraic understanding of worship is that twenty-four hours a day seven days a week we are worshiping. Every breath we take is an expression of our love for God. Whenever we are doing those things that please God (living a godly life), then we are worshiping God. The Psalmist said that God inhabits the praises of His people, which means that the Spirit of God indwells the worship of the true worshiper.

So, if living a godly life is an act of worship, a godly life will also be anointed by the Spirit of God and be empowered by God for whatever works of service the Lord may ask us to do.

But what happens if we start living an ungodly life? Well, with our Hebraic understanding of worship, we realize that whatever we are doing we are always worshiping! Now we are obeying the desires of the god of this world. We cannot, now, be worshiping the true God.

So, in reality, when we live in an ungodly way we are offering our worship, not to the true God, but to Satan, the god of this world. It is not surprising, therefore, that the spirit which can indwell people as a result of worshiping Satan is not the Holy Spirit, but an unclean spirit. This explains why deliverance ministry was such an important part of the ministry of Jesus and is still an important part of the ministry of healing and discipleship today. Jesus came to set the captives free!

Empowered by the Spirit

When Jesus went back to heaven, those first disciples would have felt very alone. They'd just received an extraordinary commission from Jesus to go into all the world and make disciples of every nation (people group) on Planet Earth! They must have looked at themselves and felt very aware of their inadequacies and lack of appropriate experience and training! For three years they had watched, encouraged and supported Jesus in His work, but now they were on their own. At least, for a short time!

Before Jesus had gone back to heaven He had told them that He would send another Comforter to be with them. He said that *"you will receive power when the Holy Spirit comes on you"* (Acts 1:8). They knew what had happened when Jesus had been baptized by John the Baptist. The heavens opened and everyone saw the Spirit of God descend on Jesus and they heard that amazing voice from heaven say, *"This is my Son, whom I love; with him I am pleased"* (Matthew 3:17). That's what happened to Jesus, but would it happen for them?

The Bible tells us that just as Jesus' ministry was initiated by a dramatic visible intervention by the Holy Spirit from heaven, so something similar happened to the disciples who were obedient to what Jesus had asked them to do. In their case the physical evidence that initiated the church era – the era in which we are still living – was of tongues of fire that came to rest on each one of them (Acts 2:3) and the sudden ability to worship God in foreign tongues as the Holy Spirit gave them the words to say (Acts 2:4).

This first Baptism in the Holy Spirit brought the Comforter, who Jesus had told them to wait for in Jerusalem. The Holy Spirit became their source of power as they used the authority God had given them to proclaim the Word of God. Simon Peter got up and preached on that first Pentecost Sunday and answered the questions people were asking about what had happened to these disciples of Jesus.

Peter told the story of Jesus (Acts 2:14–36). And when the people heard it they were crying out, *"what shall we do?"* (Acts 2:37) and Peter replied, *"Repent and be baptised, every one of you, in the name of Jesus Christ for the forgiveness of your sins. And you will receive the gift of the Holy Spirit. The promise is for you and your children and for all who are far off – for all who the Lord your God will call"* (Acts 2:38–39).

This is the promise that still holds good for today – the promise of both salvation and the promise of the Holy Spirit. It is the Holy Spirit who convicts of sin and draws us to the Savior. And it is the same Holy Spirit who then wants to pour His life into us and become the very presence of God in our lives, empowering every step of our pilgrimage with God. What an awesome privilege to be accompanied in our walk by the same presence of God Himself who came upon Jesus at the beginning of His ministry and who was then given to believers to empower the Church.

The Holy Spirit brings wonderful gifts which equip us for service as disciples of the King, including the gifts of wisdom, knowledge, faith, healings, miracles, prophecy, discernment of spirits, tongues and interpretation of tongues described in 1 Corinthians 12:7–11. And as we get to know the Lord better, the Holy Spirit will grow the amazing fruit of the Holy Spirit in our lives – the love, joy peace, patience, goodness, faithfulness, kindness, gentleness and self-control that Paul tells us about in Galatians 5:22–23.

At the end of Chapter 4 there was a prayer of salvation. If you prayed that prayer it would have been the start of your Christian life, as you were born again, or a significant moment of rededication of your life to God.

This next prayer is for the presence and the empowerment of the Holy Spirit so that you will have the presence and the power of God in and with you. You can then begin to move into your destiny as a disciple of Jesus Christ. We come to Jesus as we are, with all the issues of life that have contributed to the mess that we were in at that point of salvation. God doesn't expect us to be ready-cleaned and trained and to become an instant, perfect disciple!

But often people ask me questions such as, "How can I be filled with the Spirit like the disciples were?" There is only one relevant key – it is the key of repentance that Simon Peter held out for us in his Pentecost sermon. God doesn't look on the outer appearance, He looks on the heart. Is your heart's desire to be totally sold out to Jesus Christ and to live your life in His service? Are you sorry for your sins and wanting to turn from them (repent)? Are you determined, God being your helper, to learn to walk in God's ways as a true disciple of Jesus Christ?

If the answer to these questions is yes, you are ready to be baptized in the Holy Spirit. Here is the prayer for you to pray:

Father God, I come to You now and thank You for Jesus my Savior. I choose to turn from my sins and walk in His ways.

Jesus, I ask You to come now and baptize me in the Holy Spirit, just as You did in the early days of the Church. I ask You to fill me to overflowing with the Spirit of God.

Holy Spirit, I ask that You will give me all those gifts that I need to be a disciple of Jesus Christ and to grow in me the sweet fruit that comes from Your presence. And as I learn to be a disciple of Jesus, I ask that You will expose all unholiness and darkness in my life, so that I may be set free to serve God, empowered by the Spirit, and to do the works of the Kingdom of God.

Thank You, Jesus, for hearing and answering my prayer, Amen.

For some people, the moment they pray that prayer, or something like it, they are aware of the Holy Spirit's presence and begin to speak in tongues. For others there can be a period of waiting as they trust God, in faith, to answer the cry of their heart. For me, personally, there was a significant gap between my first praying such a prayer and the dramatic moment when I knew that God had filled me with His Spirit.

In that period between praying the prayer and being baptized in the Spirit, there were many things God was doing in my life. The most important thing was getting to the end of myself and my own abilities and realizing that it had to be all of Him and none of me!

The Discipline of Love

A true disciple welcomes discipline! And the discipline of the Lord is a ministry of love! Hebrews 12:10 says that God disciplines us in love so that we will be able to share in His holiness! If we let Him, the Holy Spirit will be our constant companion, showing us those areas of our lives which need to come under discipline, so that we may be trained in the ways of God.

A horse that has never been broken in is still a horse, but it's useless for carrying people. It's only when it has come under discipline and has learned to respond to its owner's instructions that it can ever be useful. In just the same way, we need to be *"broken in,"* and to become experienced in hearing and obeying the Master's voice. Then we will be true disciples of Jesus and will become those who are capable of doing mighty exploits in the Kingdom of God.

God's discipline never crushes or breaks our spirit. It always releases us into our destiny. It's as we put ourselves in the way of God that our ears become sensitive to the voice of God and we are then able to do the will of God.

Summary

Living according to God's standing orders for the Christian life equips us for battle and is the heart of discipleship. Being baptized in the Holy Spirit empowers us for a life of service. We are then able to be strengthened for the task and to be at all times in a place of readiness for whatever it is that God may be asking us to do.

CHAPTER 6

FORGIVENESS

The Forgiveness Issue

I will never forget a lady who came on a Healing Retreat at Ellel Grange. She only wanted prayer for her disintegrating back. She didn't want to hear me teach about forgiveness. She left in great anger. But she couldn't sleep that night and it was only when she was urged by the Lord to forgive the people that had hurt her that she got some sleep.

When she woke up in the morning she discovered that God had healed her deafness. It's amazing what God is released to do in our lives when we start to listen to His voice and do what He is asking us to do! She came back the next day and asked for prayer for her back. It was no surprise that after this testimony God healed her back as well!

In 1994 over a million people were massacred in the Rwandan genocide. Frida, a fourteen-year-old girl, was also killed, or so her attackers thought. She was thrown in the grave with the other fifteen members of her family. But fourteen hours later she was dragged out of the grave still alive.

Having escaped from Rwanda she went to school for a time
in Gabon. Later she returned to Rwanda and a Christian girl led
her to faith in Jesus. When Frida read "the Book," she discovered
that Jesus asked us to forgive those who had hurt us. So Frida
took this literally and when she returned to Rwanda she went to
the jail where the man who had killed her father was in prison to
speak out her forgiveness.

What a brave and courageous thing to do – but that simple
act has brought amazing blessing into her life. When she came on
a training school at Ellel Grange, God healed her memories of the
terrible trauma that had been a cruel curse on her life. She was
also healed of the constant head pain that had been there, ever
since she had been hit on the back of the head by those who had
killed all her family.

All disciples of Jesus will have to face the forgiveness issue
at some time in their life. It is one of those foundational principles that lies at the very heart of Christian truth. By choosing
to forgive those who have hurt us, we are consciously choosing
to remove some significant stones from the ground of our lives.
I have come to the conclusion that unforgiveness is one of the
top three issues that stand in the way of our relationship with
God, our relationship with others, even our healing and the
fruitfulness of our lives.

The Law of Sowing and Reaping

In the first chapter we saw how the physical universe is controlled by unalterable laws associated with the world God has
made. But just as there are physical laws which control the
physical universe, there are also spiritual laws which control the
spiritual universe – such as the law Paul talked about in Galatians
6:7–10, the law of sowing and reaping. What we reap is always
a consequence of what we have sown. If we sow good seed, we
reap a good harvest. If we sow bad seed, we find that the nature

of the harvest matches the seed. If we sow in unforgiveness and bitterness, then the harvest is always bad.

Men and women, as physical beings, are subject to the physical laws of the universe. But we have seen how man is not just a physical being; he has a soul and a spirit and lives at the interface of the physical and the spiritual. This means that what happens in the spiritual realms can affect the physical and what happens in the physical realms can affect the spiritual.

As children we quickly learn about the dangers of ignoring physical laws. Our parents try to protect us from discovering the law of gravity by stopping us from falling down stairs and the laws of motion by keeping us away from dangerous traffic. But where do we learn about the dangers of ignoring spiritual laws?

It was God's intention that our parents should not only teach us vital physical lessons, but also teach us equally vital spiritual lessons. For just as there can be very serious physical consequences of being ignorant of the physical laws, there can be worse consequences of being ignorant of the spiritual laws. Ignoring physical laws has a serious consequence in time, but ignoring spiritual laws can have a serious consequence in eternity!

Because of the Fall mankind lost his intuitive understanding of these spiritual principles. But God loved us so much that He gave us His written Word (the Bible) so that we could understand about spiritual things, learn what the consequences are of ignoring spiritual laws and begin to make right choices.

The Law of Forgiveness

Every one of us has free will – the ability to make choices about anything and everything in life. We can make right choices or wrong choices, good choices or bad choices. The right and good choices will bring blessing into our lives. The wrong and bad choices will have the opposite effect.

One day the disciples were asking Jesus how to pray. Jesus' answer was to give them a pattern that could form the basis of all our prayers. We call it the Lord's Prayer (Matthew 6:9–13), although in reality it was meant to be the disciples' prayer!

All who believe in God and pray naturally want to know that their sins are forgiven. They don't want their unforgiven sins to remain on God's slate for eternity and be a barrier between them and God. Therefore, it would have been a relief to the disciples to hear Jesus include within the Lord's Prayer a phrase that began, *"Forgive us our trespasses. . ."*

We trespass when we go beyond what we are allowed. If we ignore the *"Private"* signs and walk on someone else's land, we are trespassing. When we step over God's line, the line that divides right from wrong, we are trespassing against God. We leave behind our spiritual footprints – God knows where we have been!

Just as human relationships are damaged when we trespass on someone else's property, relationships with God are damaged when we trespass spiritually. Our conscience is affected and we know we've done wrong. Deep inside we long for restoration of relationship. To remedy the situation, we need to face up to our sin, deal with our pride and humbly come back to God. We need to say we are sorry and ask for forgiveness for our sin. Humility is the gateway to God's grace!

The Lord's Prayer brings us to this point of asking God for forgiveness, but then we suddenly find that the next phrase contains some initially unwelcome and challenging words! Not only does it say, *"Forgive us our trespasses,"* but it also says, *"as we forgive those who trespass against us."* It is here that we come up against one of those vital spiritual laws – laws that cannot be changed and laws that we are subject to even though we don't want to be, whether we like it or not!

The disciples must have struggled with the idea of having to forgive others as well, for Jesus had to tell them again – and in very simple words: *"if you do not forgive men their sins, your Father will not forgive your sins"* (Matthew 6:15).

Simon Peter even asked Jesus how often he needed to forgive others, suggesting that perhaps seven was a very large and generous number! There was a gentle rebuke in Jesus' words when He replied, *"No, not seven times, but seventy-times-seven"* (Matthew 18:21–22), in other words, Simon, stop counting and just keep on forgiving!

The Law of Blessing

If we want to know the continuous blessing of God, then we have to be continuously forgiving of other people. Otherwise when we ask God to forgive us, we will be asking Him for something that we are not willing to give to others. We will become trapped by our own hypocrisy! Forgiveness of sin is the greatest possible blessing that God makes available to His children, but if we are not willing to forgive others, we will miss out on God's best for our lives.

Consider the examples of Mary, Alec and Jane, who discovered the blessing that comes with forgiveness.

Mary had been sexually abused by her father for many years, but she had also done many wrong things. She had entered into several wrong sexual relationships, looking for the comfort her father should have given her and which was missing in her life.

Mary knew these relationships had been wrong and she confessed them to God with many tears. She knew she had done the right thing in confessing them, but she didn't feel much different as a result, and she couldn't understand why.

It was then that she had to face the hardest decision of her life – whether or not she would choose to forgive her own father. How could she, after he had done such terrible things to her? But deep inside she knew that it was her attitude towards her father that was a barrier which prevented her from knowing the forgiveness of God for herself.

Mary slowly faced the issue, and she realized that if she didn't forgive her father, the thoughts of what he'd done would control her for the rest of her days. She wanted to be free so much, and yet to be free, she had to give up all the bitterness and anger in her heart.

Finally the battle was won and she was able to forgive him. It was only then that she knew the full depth of God's love for her as He lifted the burden of her own sins. She was experiencing the blessing of God in a totally new way – just as Jesus had said in Matthew 6:14.

Mary had learned that we can't ignore God's spiritual law of forgiveness. It is just as powerful in the spiritual realms as the law of gravity in the physical realms. Ignore the law and we bring suffering on ourselves; abide by the law and we walk in God's blessing.

Alec struggled desperately with what he thought was the unfairness of having to forgive others – until he experienced in his heart the joy and blessing of forgiving the person who'd hurt him the most. He was then a totally different man, desperate to think of anyone else he could forgive so that he could enjoy more of the blessing!

Jane had been thrown off the back of a motorbike through the carelessness of its driver. She had landed on her head and for the past twenty-four years had suffered continuously with back pain which prevented her from doing many of the normal things of life, such as running, carrying her shopping or even holding her children.

When she asked for prayer for her bad back I started to pray, but then sensed the Lord checking me. Before I could pray I found myself asking if she had forgiven the man who'd been driving the bike. Immediately, anger and bitterness filled her face as she said, *"That man has ruined my life."* It was clear there was no forgiveness in her heart. It took a little while for one of our team to talk her through the Scriptures and for her to come to that place of agreement with what Jesus had said. But when she did so, her face was unbelievably different!

Now I prayed that Jesus would take the trauma out of her spine and set her free from the infirmity that had been her constant companion for twenty-four years. Her healing was almost immediate and the following morning she was up at 6.00 a.m. going for a run to exercise her freshly healed back. What a transformation as she returned to a perfectly normal way of life, completely healed. Forgiveness had been the radical key to permanent healing.

Mary, Alec and Jane, and thousands like them, have discovered God's spiritual laws the hard way. By ignoring the command of God to forgive, they discovered the law that bound them in spiritual chains. When they forgave, they discovered another law – this time a law of blessing. Then they began to know the forgiveness of God for themselves. They learned the relationship between forgiving others and being forgiven, and they began to taste for themselves the blessings of God's promises.

But They Don't Deserve to be Forgiven!

Sometimes righteous anger about what has happened to people becomes a permanent stumbling block to the healing of forgiveness. A deep sense of unfairness can rise up as they say words like,

"They don't deserve to be forgiven." Which is true, they don't deserve to be forgiven.

But the fact is none of us deserve to be forgiven! Jesus didn't offer us God's forgiveness through the cross because we deserved it! It was an act of grace, an act of mercy. And our forgiveness towards others has to be like that as well. It is never a matter of deserving forgiveness; it is always an act of grace and mercy.

Sometimes people say, *"But if I forgive, that means they are being let off the hook!"* It may feel like that, but it's definitely not the case. What's happening is that you are taking yourself off their hook. They are still on God's hook! They are still accountable to God for what they've done. Yes, there is restoration with God for them also, if they choose to deal with their sin before Him, in the same way as you deal with yours. But when you forgive, you're not releasing them from their responsibility towards God; you're just releasing yourself from being under the control of that person for the rest of your life.

When you forgive others – you let go! It is one of the most powerful things that you can ever do. It releases the anointing of God into your life in an unprecedented way – it brings the law of blessing into force in your life. We've seen so many people wonderfully blessed and healed as they have dug out the rocks in the ground of their lives which, until then, had a right to be there through bitterness and unforgiveness.

Getting on with the Job

Once people have understood the principle, and want to get these particular stones out of the soil of their lives, they need to make a choice and start forgiving those who have hurt them. I always encourage people to take time out to think and pray through their lives, get out a piece of paper and start making a list of those who need to be forgiven. A prayer such as the following will help prepare you for the task:

Thank You, Jesus, for teaching me the importance of forgiving others. Please help me to remember all the people who have hurt me so that I can forgive them from my heart.

Prayers like this one don't have to be long or terribly formal – God is interested in you as a person and in the decisions of your heart, not in whether or not you are good with words!

One way of making your list is to think through your life. You can begin at the beginning and work forward or you can start from where you are and work backward – it doesn't matter which. But whichever direction you decide to go, the two names that need to be at the top of your list are your parents – even if you think they were perfect!

In reality no parents were ever perfect, and they may also have carried to you problems caused by what their parents and grandparents had done. (You may also need to repent of any ungodly reactions you had to things your parents did – there are two sides to every relationship!)

Be careful and systematic, and give God a chance to remind you of people you might have forgotten. Every time you think of someone you need to forgive, write down his or her name. You may also find it helpful to write down the particular reason for which you need to forgive that person. You need to ask God to remind you of things that may have happened in your family, with your friends and with any other circle of people with whom you have shared something of your life over the years.

Think back on every year of your life and everywhere you've been – school, work, church, sports events, vacations, and so on. Don't rush it – give yourself space and time. Some names will cause you more pain than others, and you might even have difficulty writing down some of the names. Inside you might think that you don't want to forgive them or they don't deserve to be forgiven, but remember, you've made a decision to forgive, so ask God to help you write down those names!

As you go down the list, pray carefully over each name. Remind yourself for a moment about what it was they did to you, and then pray something like this:

> *I now choose to forgive Chris [insert the name of the person you are forgiving] for what he/she did to me. I now release him/her into the freedom of my forgiveness. I will not hold these things against him/her anymore.*

As you pray through your list from the heart, you will find that God slowly changes you from the inside out. You will be leaving behind all the bad things that resentment and bitterness have brought into your life and begin to emerge like a butterfly at the beginning of a new era.

Finally, ask God to set you free from all the chains that previously bound you to all these people. You can use a prayer something like this:

> *Thank You, Lord, for helping me forgive all these people [give a single name if you pray this prayer for one person at a time]. I ask now that You set me free from every ungodly influence they have had on my life and every hold that Satan has had on my life through what they did. Please cut the ropes that have held me tightly to the pain of the past and set me free to serve You.*

And Don't Forget to Forgive Yourself!

When we have made mistakes, got something terribly wrong, or tragedies have happened as a result of things we've done, people will often say, *"I'll never forgive myself for . . ."* They fill in the gap with details of whatever it was, as if that should be the end of the matter.

But when we refuse to forgive ourselves we are also cutting ourselves off from God's blessing on our lives. Jesus died that we might be forgiven. Nothing we've done is so awful that it's not covered by what Jesus did for us on the cross. And if, therefore, God is able to forgive us and we say, *"I will never forgive myself,"* we are putting ourselves above God.

So don't forget to put your own name on the list, if you struggle with the consequences of mistakes you have made or have ever cursed yourself by saying something like, *"I'll never forgive myself!"*

Summary

Not forgiving others is one of the biggest stumbling blocks to making progress with living life God's way! As soon as we understand that there's a spiritual law attached to forgiveness and we choose to listen to what Jesus said on the subject and put what He said into practice, the sooner we will be able to empty the soil of our lives of some of the biggest stones that the enemy can use to limit our potential in the Kingdom of God.

CHAPTER 7

BUILDING ON A GOOD FOUNDATION

Many years ago I lectured at Manchester University on Building Science and Technology. My specialty was building defects! This gave me plenty of opportunity to study buildings that had failed and find out what had happened. Later, in my publishing career, I published a book called *Building Disasters and Failures*.

Some buildings fail because their design was at fault, others because the concrete wasn't strong enough for the job, but the overwhelming majority of building failures come about because the foundations were inadequate for the weight of the building. The building would settle into the ground, causing cracks to the superstructure, often meaning that demolition was the only sensible course of action.

Jesus was a carpenter and builder by profession. His specialty was making things out of wood. But it is obvious that He knew a thing or two about buildings. At the end of His Sermon on the Mount (Matthew 5, 6 and 7) He sums up this all-important teaching by telling a story of two builders (Matthew 7:24–27). Jesus had probably witnessed something very like the story He was about to tell. The story is designed to illustrate the difference between someone who takes note of Jesus' teaching and puts it into practice and someone who ignores it and builds their life according to their own understanding.

In the story two men are each building a house for themselves. One is described as being wise and the other as foolish. The wise man built his house on a solid rock foundation, whereas the other chose what must have been a more attractive location. In spite of the absence of rock beneath the surface of the ground, he chose to build his house on the sandy foundation of his preferred building site.

Everything was fine until the weather changed. In the Middle East the weather can be constantly good for many months, even years. But when it rains, it can rain so hard that the roads become rivers in a very short space of time. And in Jesus' story the rain came down, the streams rose, and the winds blew and beat against those two houses! The house that was built on the rock stood firm and was unaffected by the weather. There was no loose sand under the foundations to be washed away and undermine the walls. But the house that was built on sand suffered total collapse.

Jesus used this dramatic illustration to compare the lives of those who build on a good and solid foundation and those who have little or no concern for the way they are living. And the measure that Jesus used to determine who was wise and who was foolish was simply whether or not they were obedient to the things Jesus had taught. It is clear from the story that both builders heard the teaching, but only one of them put it into practice.

Psalm 19:7 tells us that *"The statutes of the Lord are trustworthy, making wise the simple."* It is tragically true that many of the cleverest and most gifted people in the world finish up making shipwreck of their personal lives, because they choose to live life their own way instead of God's way. They ignore the statutes of the Lord and have no respect for God's Law. On a daily basis the newspapers are full of the ever-changing relationships, the drug- and alcohol-induced life-styles and the tragedies of many types that seem to happen so often to the rich and famous.

Parental Influence

People are accountable for the damage they do to themselves as a result of their ungodly choices. Sadly, however, the damage they do is not restricted solely to their own lives. Would that it was! In God's original plan He put people into families, so that as children grow up they would learn about God from their parents and learn to love and respect God from their parents' example. But when parents turn away from living their lives according to godly principles, it's not just the parents that suffer. The bad example that has been set for the children often becomes the marker by which they determine their own lives and actions. As a result there is often a decline in morality from one generation to another.

The Ten Commandments express this principle so succinctly. In Exodus 20:5 it says that the sins of the fathers will be visited on the children. And when parenting fails, eventually society will bear the cost of such failure, and even the laws of the land will be modified to suit the changing morality of the electorate.

It's not just the Bible that states such truth, however. The London *Daily Telegraph* of the 11th April 2008 contained these words, *"When our legal system loses its moral compass, it is only to be expected that on the streets of Britain many impressionable children will do the same."* As I am typing these very words into my computer, the papers are full of another teenage murder on our streets. A sixteen-year-old boy was violently killed in a cake shop. He is one of many young people that have died on the streets of Britain in recent months.

In another town there is an epidemic of teenage suicides – over twenty in just a few months. What a terrible ending to young lives who have been betrayed by their parents' generation and been seduced by the voice of the enemy in their own. People without foundations are in danger of raising children without hope. I am so thankful to God for my parents, who saw it as their primary responsibility to teach their children to live in the love and the fear of the Lord.

The evidence of my own country is, sadly, typical of many nations around the world. In spite of the fact that British law was largely founded on Judeo-Christian principles, Christian morality is no longer politically correct and our law-makers are steadily eliminating the Christian influence. The nation will suffer as a result.

Integrity seems to be a thing of the past; over 200,000 abortions are carried out every year; there is little discipline among the young and our city streets have become places of fear and danger. Drugs, sexual license and violence have become the way of life for so many. TV and internet pornography has become the entertainment of the masses, destroying respect for the bodies God gave us and for many it has eliminated shame from the consequences of sin. And the extent of relationship breakdown is such that 50 per cent of our children are being brought up in one-parent families. We are raising a generation of fatherless children, many of whom have no stable and loving discipline with which to form a spiritual backbone based on the wisdom of God. The spiritual foundations of the nation are no longer adequate to face the storms that will come.

Over a century ago, in 1877, Richard Dugdale researched the generational history of one family in New York – the descendants of Max Jukes, who was born at the beginning of the eighteenth century. He lived and died at approximately the same time in history as Jonathan Edwards, the great evangelist and preacher. When Dugdale compared the two family lines of generational descendants he came up with some remarkable statistics.

Max Jukes lived in New York, he did not believe in Jesus Christ and opposed Christian teachings. He refused to take his children to church, even when they wanted to attend. By 1877, he had 1,026 descendants. Of these:

300 were sent to prison for an average of 13 years each

190 were public prostitutes

680 were admitted alcoholics

27 were murderers

By 1877 his family had cost the state of New York in excess of $1.25 million in 19th century dollars (probably at least a 100 times this amount in today's money). With few exceptions none of his children made any worthwhile contribution to society.

The contrast with the generational line of Jonathan Edwards could not be starker or more demonstrative of the truth of Jesus' parable about the need for having good foundations:

Jonathan Edwards loved the Lord and was a great man of God. He saw to it that his children attended church, even if they did not want to. By 1877 he had 929 descendants. Of these:

430 were ministers

86 became university professors

13 became university presidents

75 became authors

5 were elected to Congress

2 were elected to the Senate

3 were State Governors

1 became Vice President of the United States

His family had made a tremendous contribution to society and there is no record of any one of the descendants of the Edwards family having become a liability to the Government!

Building foundations into the lives of our children will always produce a rich reward, both for the family and for the nation.

The prophet Hosea saw how the lack of spiritual foundations was destroying the land and destroying the nation. In Hosea chapter 4, the prophet bemoans the fact that there is no faithfulness, love or acknowledgment of God in the land – only cursing, lying, murder, stealing and adultery. He could have been describing the headlines from today's newspapers!

People no longer have any respect for God's law (they break all bounds) and bloodshed follows bloodshed (could be wars, famine and abortions). Because of this, Hosea then says, *"the land mourns, and all who live in it waste away; the beasts of the field and the birds of the air and the fish of the seas are dying."* Hosea is describing an environmental disaster in language which is reminiscent of today's green campaigners. Then he sums up the situation by giving God's perspective on it all in chapter 4:6: *"my people are destroyed from lack of knowledge"* which brings us back to Jesus' teaching from the Sermon on the Mount.

It has been our experience down the years to discover that this prevailing situation can also exist inside the Church. Many of those who come for help on Healing Retreats and Training Courses have been destroyed because of lack of knowledge of God's ways and God's laws. So often, people have wept out their anguish and frustration at their church leaders, who have failed to warn of the dangers when they were young. Now, a generation later, they are paying the price of having no foundations to their very lives.

Is There Any Hope?

It is easy to look at passages like this one in Hosea, see the mess the world is in and want to give up! But the Word of God is also full of wonderful promises of the blessings God longs to pour out on His people who choose to walk in fellowship and relationship with Him. In Deuteronomy 28 the blessings of obeying the commandments of God are spelled out as part of the Old Covenant blessings. Everything is embraced by the blessing of God – family, business, livestock, land – this was God's intention for His children.

At the beginning of the Sermon on the Mount, in the New Testament, more blessings are spoken of by Jesus for those who keep their eye and their heart on Kingdom principles rather than their own interests. Those who are "poor in spirit" (don't allow their own selfish desires to become more important than God's best for their lives) are promised the Kingdom of Heaven. Those who mourn will be comforted, the meek will inherit the earth and those who hunger and thirst after righteousness will be filled.

Later in the Sermon Jesus tackles the subject of adultery and also makes the very telling comment that those who look on a woman to lust after her have already committed adultery with her in their heart (Matthew 5:28). And when we read that God judges the thoughts and intentions of the heart (Hebrews 4:12) we realize why permissiveness in all its forms is so undermining of a godly society and opens the door to every other form of sin and perversion.

In Chapter 6:22, Jesus describes the eye as the lamp of the body and says that if our eyes are good, then the whole body will be full of light, but if our eyes are bad, that our whole body will be full of darkness. Here Jesus is directly saying that if we dwell with our eyes on the ungodly and the lustful, then we are opening up our body, which God intended to be the temple of the Holy Spirit, to the darkness of Satan's power and control. Jesus touches on many other things in the sermon – everything from loving our enemies, to anxiety, worry and being generous with our giving. What an amazing guide to the foundations of Christian living!

On reading through these three chapters you will come to the conclusion that it is impossible for human beings to follow the standards Jesus set without divine help. For every single one of us is tainted by the sin of mankind and has a carnal nature. The carnal nature will always lead us away from God and into the deceptive traps of the enemy. Two things are needed to prevent this happening. We must have self-control by the power of the Holy Spirit and we need the discipling (discipline) which comes from those whom God gives to us to support and encourage us in the Christian life.

The book of Proverbs encourages us to train up a child in the way that he should go, for when he is old he will not depart from it. Discipline and training for children produces wonderful rewards. In just the same way, when a person becomes a Christian, they are like a child, they are young in the faith and they are in need of training. When new Christians, of all ages, come into the faith through the gateway of repentance and are filled with the Spirit and then properly discipled in the ways of the Kingdom, then there is no limit to what God can do through the life of any one believer.

The whole of this book and, of course, the DVD series of programs and the Study Guide are all designed to help you in your walk of faith, through building your life on a solid foundation, preparing you for the destiny that God has chosen for you. In the next two chapters we will be looking at how God is able to start putting solid foundations into our lives through the Scriptures and prayer.

The Psalmist summed up this objective perfectly when he said: *"My soul finds rest in God alone; my salvation comes from him. He alone is my rock and my salvation; he is my fortress, I shall never be shaken"* (Psalm 62:1–2). We need not fear the storms or the attacks the enemy may throw at us if we are thoroughly grounded in the rock of our salvation!

Summary

Without solid foundations not only will buildings fail, but believers will be in danger of walking away from their faith. There are many things listed by Paul in Galatians 5:16–21 and Ephesians 5:17–6:21, which are not right for believers to be involved with. It is only by having solid foundations that we will be able to stand when temptations and testings come our way.

CHAPTER 8

FEEDING ON THE LIVING BREAD

Living Food and Drink!

Food is essential for life. Eat the right food and the body grows strong and healthy. Our dietary system is a chemical processing plant which is designed to extract the good things from our food supply and distribute them to the various organs of our body. What's not wanted is eliminated in the usual ways.

There are some things our bodies are not designed to process. If we eat non-food items they could make us very ill. And then there are those things which are poisonous because we have no means of either processing them or eliminating them. If we eat poisoned food we could die! And if we happen to be stung or bitten by a venomous creature such as a snake, unless there is an antidote readily available, it can be fatal.

Because our bodies react quickly to the nature of food, we have a very quick measure of what is good or bad for us and we are careful, therefore, not to eat things that make us ill. We do not like the experience of being ill and avoid such foods at all cost.

In Chapter 2 we looked carefully at how God made each of us as three-dimensional human beings – with a body, a soul and a spirit. It is certainly important that we are careful about our physical food and remain physically healthy. But it is even more important that we feed our spirit and soul with good food also. Jesus referred to Himself as *"the Bread of Life"* and said, *"He who comes to me will never grow hungry and he who believes in me will never be thirsty"* (John 6:35).

Obviously Jesus is not speaking here about people eating His physical body, or obtaining from Him an endless supply of liquid water. The woman at the well in John 4 made that mistake. When Jesus told her of the water supply that would be in her as a never-failing stream, she immediately thought of physical water and asked Jesus for a supply so that she wouldn't need to keep on coming to the well to draw water!

On both these occasions Jesus is talking about food for the spirit and the soul – food and drink that will never run out. As a child we sang many choruses which were designed to teach biblical truths in a simple way. One of my favorites was:

I'm feeding on the living bread,
I'm drinking at the fountain head;
And whoso drinketh, Jesus said
Shall never, never thirst again.
What, never thirst again?
No! Never thirst again.
What, never thirst again?
No! Never thirst again.
And whoso drinketh, Jesus said,
Shall never, never thirst again.

I must have been no more than five or six years of age when first I learned these words. And I've never forgotten them. Nor have I ever forgotten the significance of their meaning. I didn't understand then about spirit, soul and body, but I did know that when I read the Bible I was both eating and drinking spiritual food and refreshment which would stand me in good stead for the rest of my life.

I was keen to learn about Jesus for I knew He mattered so much to my Mum and Dad. I knew He must be very important! It wasn't until I was nine years old that I knelt by my bedside with my father and invited Jesus into my heart to be my Savior. I understood what I was doing and I suspect there were a few tears of thanksgiving shed by my Mum and Dad that night after they had tucked me up in bed! It was a moment I have never forgotten and never regretted.

Every day I would read both a portion of Scripture and the Scripture Union Junior Notes. I'm sure there was much I didn't understand, but because I got it into my system when I was young, much of it is still there now that I am very much older. Well over sixty years have passed, and I am still drawing on the resources that were put into my spiritual bank account in those early days of my life! The Bible is food for the spirit and food for the soul and if we adhere to the scriptural principles of living it will prove to be good for the body as well!

But just as there is good food for the spirit and soul there is also a huge amount of bad food out there in today's world – food that enters through the eyes and ears and impacts our very being. The things we read, hear and look at can bring either blessing or curse into our lives.

When we dwell on bad things like occult literature and films, immoral or pornographic material, gruesome and violent stories, then we are corrupting our souls and damaging our spirit. It is the equivalent for the soul of the body swallowing poisonous food. Even Job recognized the dangers of looking lustfully at a girl, for example, when he said in Job 31:1, *"I made a covenant with my eyes not to look lustfully at a girl"* and then in the fourth verse, *"Does he*

[God] not see my ways and count my every step?" Then in the seventh
verse Job expresses understanding that our heart can be led astray
by our eyes!

It is so important that we guard our lives from the intake of
all types of poisonous food. The Bible is the best soul food available. If we feed on the spiritual truths that are so clearly taught
there it will both satisfy our soul and at the same time introduce
Holy Spirit inspired truth into our beings. It will build us up in
our relationship with God and alert us to danger when we are
tempted to read or look at the blatantly ungodly.

Psalm 119:9 expresses it this way, *"How can a young man keep
his way pure? By living according to your word."* Then in verse 11, *"I
have hidden your word in my heart that I might not sin against you."*
And in verse 105 we read, *"Your word is a lamp to my feet and a light
for my path."*

So What Actually is the Bible?

In outline the Bible is the record of the people of God from the
creation right through to the foundation of the Church. And in
prophecy the Bible also embraces the second coming of Jesus, the
end of the world and the final judgment.

In the Old Testament we have the special story of the children of Abraham, Isaac and Jacob – the Jewish people, through
whom God chose to reveal Himself to the world and, in due
time, give birth to the Messiah. In the New Testament we have
the birth of the Messiah, the story of Jesus and the founding of
the Church.

The Bible is the most amazing of books. It is not just one
book, but a compendium of sixty-six different books, written by
forty different authors over sixteen centuries. But it was the same
Holy Spirit who inspired every single one of the authors – hence
the incredible unity of vision, purpose and content, as the truth

about God is progressively revealed through its pages and all the authors support one another in what they have written.

The Bible also contains an astonishing variety of literary styles. There are stories about the lives of good and bad people and what happened to them, accounts of battles, journeys, the life of Jesus and the story of the early Church. There are also many letters written to groups of Christians which contain vital teaching from people like the Apostles Paul and Peter. It comes to us in narratives and dialogue, in proverbs and parables, in songs and allegories, in history and prophecy.

Looking at the Bible from a different perspective, we find as believers that:

It is God's revelation to man of the truth about Himself. It is, therefore, the most precious book ever written.

It is a guide for living life to the full. It gives us a road map for the perilous journey of life. Or to put it another way, on our voyage through life's ocean, we find our anchor right here.

It is a storehouse of wonderful stories for children and grown-ups. Remember Noah and the ark? Joseph's coat of many colors? Daniel in the lions' den? Jonah and the fish? The parables of Jesus? In these stories we recognize the triumphs and failures of ordinary people – and we may even see ourselves!

It is a refuge in time of trouble. People in pain, in suffering, in prison, in mourning, tell how they turned to the Bible and found strength there in their desperate hours.

It is a treasury of insight as to who we are. We are not meaningless robots, but we are magnificent creatures of a God who loves us and gives us a purpose and a destiny.

It is a sourcebook for everyday living. We find standards for our conduct, guidelines for knowing right from wrong, and principles to help us in a confused society where so often "anything goes."

Above all *it contains the keys of Salvation.*

Victor Hugo, the famous French novelist, said that the people of England are a people of two books, the Bible and Shakespeare. He then said that England made Shakespeare, but the Bible made England. But the tragedy today is that the people of England have turned their back on their heritage that was shaped by the Bible and the God of the Bible. They are no longer a people of the Book and today's generations are reaping the consequences.

But while man can be and is unfaithful to our God of covenant faithfulness, God will never break His covenant of love with all those who come to Him and walk in humility before Him.

Paul's Assessment of the Old Testament

When Paul was writing his letters, the only Scriptures believers had were the books of the Old Testament. Some Christians today rather hastily put them on one side, saying that we are New Testament believers and they give little attention to the amazing truths about God and His dealings with men that are contained within the pages of the first part of our Bible.

Paul described them in 2 Timothy 3:15–17 in these words: *". . .the holy Scriptures, which are able to make you wise for salvation through faith in Christ Jesus. All Scripture is God-breathed and is useful for teaching, rebuking, correcting and training in righteousness, so that the man of God may be thoroughly equipped for every good work."*

What an extraordinary commendation these words are about the Old Testament Scriptures. But it's no different than the commendation of Jesus. On the road to Emmaus, after the resurrection, He opened up the Old Testament Scriptures which spoke about Him.

With such strong encouragement from Jesus and Paul to value the Old Testament Scriptures, it would be depriving ourselves of living bread and water for our soul to ignore them. Then, of course we need to read and dwell on the Scriptures in the New Testament which speak of Jesus, the work of the Spirit and life in the Church.

How to Read the Bible

Christians are uniquely privileged when reading the Bible. They are the only people on the face of the planet who can freely chat with the author of their favorite book about what it means! To pray before reading your Bible is a great way to begin any time of reading the Bible.

The whole of Psalm 119 is about the Word and the Law of God and how precious it is. There are many prayers scattered through the Psalm which form an excellent basis for prayer before reading the Bible. Prayers such as:

Psalm 119:18: *"Open my eyes that I may see wonderful things in your law."*
Psalm 119:34: *"Give me understanding, and I will keep your law and obey it with all my heart."*

Prayer and Bible reading can't be separated. In the next chapter we will be opening up the whole subject of prayer so that Bible reading and prayer will become the foundational disciplines of our Christian walk. Our daily activities and visions for life flow from Bible reading and prayer.

A good basic rule for reading the Bible is simply this: pray before you read, pray as you read and pray about what you have read! In this way your spirit will constantly be alert to hear the voice of God speaking to you through His Word. Have a marker pen in your hand as you read, so that you can underline the particular things God says to you each day. Your Bible will then become a personal handbook for life, drawn up personally for you by God. What a privilege!

Bible Reading Programs

There are many different Bible reading programs available. These will take you through the whole of the Bible in one or two years. It's good to have the discipline of following a program like this for it ensures that we leave nothing out. And many of these programs have personal study notes to go with them, ensuring that you are not only reading the Bible, but learning from the experience of others at the same time.

Some people, however, don't feel they have the time to read the Bible passages and so they finish up just reading the notes instead. While this may be helpful, it is no substitute for reading the Word for yourself. Second-hand reading tends to make second-class Christians. There's no substitute for the real thing. It's like asking someone else to eat a meal for you, asking them to tell you what it tasted like and expecting the meal they ate to nourish your own body!

In addition to reading the Bible in this way, I urge you to read great chunks of it at a time, so that you can take in the breadth of history or prophecy that sections of the Bible contain. Keep your pen handy at all times, for you never know when the Holy Spirit is going to suddenly arrest you with understanding and revelation. When that happens it's important to make a note of it – either in the margin of your Bible or on a separate pad.

You may not understand it all – but that's OK. But if you get it in, then the Holy Spirit will get it out as and when you need it. At the right time He will give you understanding of what you need to know. Even today I can be teaching and suddenly remember an important Scripture to illustrate what I'm saying.

I just speak out the Scripture and often people will say it was such interjections in the teaching which were exactly what the person needed to hear.

But God can only do that if you have taken the time to read the Word and digest it. It has to become part of you, it is living bread, speaking of all that Jesus is, the very Bread of Life. Then, the Holy Spirit can prompt you to draw treasures out of your heart – treasure that you have hidden away in times past and which you rediscover just at the point of need.

Learning Scripture

I'm not very religious – even though I am passionate about the importance of our relationship with God. By saying I'm not very religious, I mean I am not very good with all sorts of rules, regulations and traditions which seem to have little relevance to actually living the Christian life.

I do, nevertheless, believe it's very valuable to learn some Scriptures off by heart – so that their truths become part of the person you are. That may sound a bit religious, but I can assure you that for me personally there are many times when the Scriptures I have learned earlier in life suddenly come to mind at critical times of my life. I'm so grateful that I was always encouraged to learn verses of Scripture as a child, both in Sunday School and at home with my parents.

If we take the words of the Psalmist seriously, and believe that hiding God's Word in our heart will, indeed, be an encouragement not to sin, then we dare not be undisciplined in our attitude to Scripture – we need to make it part of us!

Summary

The Bible is the most extraordinary book on the planet! It is the very Word of God to the human race. If we read it and apply its truths into our lives, it will be totally life-transforming. Every believer needs to take some time out every day to read something from its pages. The instruction to "read, mark, learn and inwardly digest" is never applied more suitably than to the Word of God. All of us need to guard our hearts by taking in something each day from the Bible.

CHAPTER 9

DYNAMIC PRAYING

For many Christians prayer is a mystery! They know it's important, because Jesus prayed a lot and because He taught the disciples how to pray, using what we call the Lord's Prayer – which was really a prayer for the disciples to use. But as far as their own prayer life is concerned it is sometimes almost non-existent – not because they don't want to pray, but because they've never learnt how to pray!

Because people have become used to listening to leaders praying in church, many have often concluded that because they can't pray like that, they will leave the praying to other people! But God intended prayer to be a dynamic reality for every one of His children; a 24-hour form of communication with Father God. Yes, there are the formal times when groups of believers are together, but it is the informal times of fellowship and communication that are at the heart of an effective and meaningful prayer life.

Believing Prayer

As a child I heard my father pray – often. He would pray in the morning and in the evening, grace before meals often got turned into an impromptu prayer time and it was obvious as I grew up that at many times during the day prayer was a normal reality of everyday life. He was a busy man with many responsibilities, both at work and in church life, but Dad always involved God in everything he was doing. Hearing how God had answered the many prayers of my parents – often for us, their children – was an unforgettable lesson for life.

Not only did I absorb the importance of prayer in the family, I was also brought up on amazing stories of how God answered the prayers of missionary saints in far-off lands. My great-uncle had a lifelong commitment to pray for the work of the China Inland Mission (CIM), founded by Hudson Taylor. Many missionaries went out to China, inspired by Uncle Will's prayers and commitment. On one occasion a lady missionary, who was home on furlough, was telling how God had protected them when carrying some money that had been given to the mission. She had to cross a range of hills to deposit the money in a bank.

After completing the assignment and having slept for a night in the hills en route, she was accosted by a man who challenged her about the soldiers that were guarding her camp that night. He had wanted to rob them of their money, but couldn't because of twenty-three soldiers who had surrounded her, her companion and their donkeys as they slept. She told him she had no soldiers and depended totally on the protection of her God.

When recounting this story back in Bolton, Uncle Will asked her what the date of this encounter had been. He kept meticulous records of every prayer meeting for the CIM and when they compared notes, Uncle Will was not surprised to discover that there had been twenty-three people present at the CIM prayer meeting the previous evening. I was impressed, not only by the fact that God answers prayer but that He answers prayers that people had not even been praying! At the meeting they had no knowledge of the event, but God saw their hearts as they prayed for this missionary and accurately reflected the attendance at the meeting in the answer to their general prayers for her protection. I have no doubt that twenty-three of the angels of the Lord encamped around that little bundle of humanity on the Chinese hills that night.

Stories like this, many of them, seriously impacted my life. I knew that God was alive and well and not just sitting in heaven ignoring events on Planet Earth, but was deeply concerned to hear and answer the prayers of His children. It's no wonder I grew up believing in prayer.

Prayer and Vision

Another vital prayer lesson I learned from Dad was that when God shows you something in vision, then prayer and action together (the faith and works of James 2:20) are the means through which God brings those things to pass. God didn't save millions of Chinese people by Hudson Taylor praying for them in England, it only happened when Hudson Taylor added action to his faith and actually went to share the reality of the gospel with Chinese people face to face.

I am daily reminded of this lesson as I look at my hands. On my little finger I wear the prayer covenant ring that was given to one CIM missionary (William Grundy) by my grandfather and my great-uncle as he sailed for Shanghai from Liverpool in 1895 in answer to the call for action as well as faith. William Grundy wore it through all his years in China as Uncle Will's CIM prayer meeting faithfully prayed him through his years of service.

One day I was teaching an Ellel Ministries school on the history of missions when God reminded me of this ring and encouraged me to wear it as a daily reminder of God's faithfulness in answering prayer and the fact that now, in my generation, Ellel Ministries is part of the answer to the prayers of the family, for well over a 100 years, for the Chinese peoples. Even as I type these words into my computer another of the Ellel leaders is conducting a special ten-day training school for Chinese people in Bangkok, Thailand.

All these prayer lessons became very important for me personally when God gave me the vision for the work of Ellel Ministries. On one, never-to-be-forgotten, day the Lord showed me that I was to spend the rest of my life ministering healing to those in need and teaching others how to do it. That vision has never gone stale – it is always fresh, new every morning.

But for ten years after receiving the vision, it was as if nothing happened – at least nothing obvious. Those ten years were, for me personally, a lonely wilderness experience of trusting God in prayer for what He had shown, even though there was nothing obvious to show for it. It is only with hindsight that I can look back and see how many of the experiences I had during those very years, became a foundation in my life for the future ministry. I was learning another very important prayer lesson – that of perseverance and endurance. There is often a considerable period of time between God's heaven-sent vision and man's earthly fulfillment – time during which prayer is the key that eventually unlocks destiny.

God heard the prayers and when the work of Ellel Ministries eventually started in 1986, we began by praying with people about the issues in their lives. The prayer lessons of life were now being lived out in the dynamic of one-to-one ministry and God began to change lives – often radically. Yes, we still had a lot of lessons to learn, and yes, we didn't get everything right, but little by little we learnt from a loving heavenly Father how much He loved His children and wanted to see them healed and their lives restored. Now, over thirty years later, there are Ellel Ministries' bases on every continent – all fulfilling the original vision to bring healing to those in need and to teach and train the Body of Christ how to do it. God has been so faithful.

The work was birthed in prayer through a regular Prayer Support Group. Every day at our Centers the teams worship and pray together and every month there are over a 100 different prayer support groups meeting to pray for the work in different parts of the world. Prayer really does change things and prepare the way for God to perform miracles.

What is Your Perspective of God?

Sometimes people find it hard to pray because they don't have a right understanding of the character and nature of God. Often, our view of what God is like is formed by our view of what our human father is like. I will never forget the woman who spat out the words, "If God's like my 'old man,' I don't want to know Him."

Her childhood experience was of a human father who had beaten and cruelly punished them without cause. So her adult perspective of God was that He was just like her human father, waiting to beat her into submission. Some fathers are just absent, perhaps they have left home for good, or are so absorbed in their business that they don't have time for the children. A child in these circumstances can easily learn from this that God isn't interested in me.

Now, it's hard to think of talking with someone who is either cruel or not interested in you, so the very idea of prayer presents huge spiritual barriers to people in these circumstances. The Bible tells us that one of the things that Jesus came to do was to show us what the Father is like. Then we could correct our misunderstandings about the nature of God and relate with Him as He desires.

We learn from the Scriptures that God is holy, loving, righteous, forgiving, accepting (even when we've done wrong), generous and wants us to know His blessing and direction throughout our lives. In fact, Jesus is just like Father God. So

when we see Jesus loving and caring for people, we know Father
God does as well. And when Jesus told the story of the prodigal
son to illustrate how Father God wants to welcome back those
who are sorry for their sin, we can know that we are included
in His loving mercy. Once we have understood these things it is
much easier to come to Him in prayer, because we know that we
can trust Him.

What is Prayer?

There are many different types of prayer, but at its simplest,
prayer is just a means of communication between a loving God
and His creation. And just as between any two people there are
many different types of communication, there are many different
types of communication between man and God. Here are some
of them with some Scriptures for you to look up as well.

Adoration and worship (John 4:21–24). I can simply be thankful
in my heart for who He is. I can look at His creation and worship
the Creator. I can look at a sunset and rejoice at the wonders He
has made.

Waiting on the Lord (Psalm 40:1–3). A waiter in a restaurant is
there to be attentive to the needs of the diners. As we wait on
the Lord we are choosing to serve Him with everything we are.

Interceding for others (Romans 8:26–29). For many people this
is all that prayer is – praying for God to intervene for good in
another person's life. It is a vital part of prayer, but if we miss out
on all the other aspects of prayer we won't really grasp what it is
He wants us to pray for in the lives of others.

Asking God for our needs (Matthew 6:7–15). God is a Father who
longs to bless His children. So just like a child comes to dad to
ask him for things we can come to our heavenly Dad in the same
way. But just as our earthly dad may say No – because he knows
it wouldn't be good for us just now – there are times when God

is not able to answer our prayers in the way we would like. This is where it is so important to be able to trust Him.

Listening to God (Proverbs 1:23). If someone tries to have a conversation with you, but never pauses for breath, it is not a conversation! Listening is as much a part of conversation as talking is. In the same way, when we pray it is very important that we spend time just being in the presence of God and learn to recognize His voice. A good way of doing this is to read the Bible, His Word, and ask God to show you things for your life out of what the Holy Spirit prompted people to put into the Bible. (See Chapter 8.)

Standing in spiritual warfare (Ephesians 6:10–18). Sometimes we are very conscious that there is spiritual opposition coming from the enemy to the things God wants to do in our lives or that He wants us to do for Him. These are times when we need to be resisting all the temptations and attacks of the enemy in prayer. We need to press forward in faith, knowing that He will strengthen and encourage us (give us courage!).

Asking God for forgiveness (1 John 1:9). Not even the greatest saint always gets everything right. And when we get things wrong, we need to come to God as soon as we're aware of what has happened, express our sorrow and ask for forgiveness. The promise of God's Word is secure and trustworthy. He WILL forgive us and cleanse us. But, just as in any human relationship, if there is something between two people that has not been resolved, the whole relationship from that point on is different, so it is with God. When there is something between us and Him, there's a barrier that has to be overcome. Jesus died that we might be forgiven, so if we don't come to Him for restoration we are not receiving the blessing that Jesus won for us on the cross.

Thanking God (1 Thessalonians 5:18). When someone gives you something it is totally natural to express your thanks to them for what they have given. It would be very bad manners not to thank them! People can sometimes forget that an important part of prayer is thanksgiving to God for all His love and provision for us.

Praising God in all circumstances – a sacrifice of praise (Hebrews 13:15). Even when circumstances are difficult, and they often will be, for we're living in a fallen and broken world where bad things do happen, we can still praise God for who He is, for His love, for His mercy and for His forgiveness. Praise is a wonderful key which can unlock the door of misery and depression, sadness and despair. Just as you are blessed when people praise you for what you have done, we can bless God by praising Him. And God responds to heartfelt praise with giving us more of His love and the presence of His indwelling Spirit.

How to Pray

Paul encouraged people to think of prayer as something that's happening all the time! He said, "Pray at all times." I believe this means we should grow so much in our relationship with God that we're always conscious of His presence and we're alert to listen to Him and talk to Him at any time of day or night.

Often, in the middle of all sorts of things that can be going on in my life, I become aware of something God is putting on my heart. I immediately turn that into a form of prayer. Jesus never did anything without His Father showing Him what to do, He always consulted His Father over what He was to say or where He was to go. If that was normal for Jesus, the Son of God, it should certainly be our objective. We need to develop a 24-hour God consciousness so that prayer becomes the vital breath of the Christian life.

But in addition to this continuous awareness of God, we also need to develop the discipline of spending specific times with Him. For this we will need to find a specific time and place when we know we can be alone with God. It's always helpful to read some Scripture as part of our prayer time, so that we allow what the Holy Spirit has written in the Word of God to become a focus of our attention as we enter the presence of God. The Bible reading can become a source of inspiration for things to pray about as well.

Using the Lord's Prayer is also a good way to be disciplined in our praying. We can just say the prayer, but it's much more effective to meditate on each part of the prayer and deal with any issues that the Holy Spirit prompts us about. For example, there may be people we need to forgive or specific things we need to pray for.

I have always found it a helpful discipline to keep a record of the major things that God leads me to pray about. During those precious days when God was envisioning me with the work I am now doing, I kept a daily diary of things that I had brought before the Lord. I can look back now and see the amazing ways in which God has answered those many prayers. What an encouragement it is to see that a loving heavenly Father has really been interested in me, one of His children!

Summary

God has created us in such a way that we are able to communicate and enjoy relationship with Him. Prayer is the means of doing this. If we learn how to pray we will never be alone. Wherever God sends us in the world to serve Him, He will always be with us and as we stay close to Him, through our prayers He will lead and direct our steps, encourage us and enable us to fulfill the destiny He has for each one of our lives.

CHAPTER 10

WEEDING MY PATCH!

The first time I became aware of God's vision for the work of Ellel Ministries, I was working on the restoration of an old car – an Alvis Speed 20. After stripping everything off the chassis, I discovered that the chassis was bent. I was heart-broken, because a car with a bent chassis is un-driveable.

As I looked at this broken car, I sensed the voice of God saying to me, *"You could restore this broken car, but I can restore broken lives."* Then He asked me a question, *"Which is more important – broken cars or broken lives?"*

Of course, the answer was obvious, but God used that situation to envision me. I began to understand that not only does God want us to know Him, so that one day we will enter heaven's glory to be with Him for ever, but He also wants to restore us so that we can be the people God wants us to be.

In a very real sense our lives are our own responsibility. They are like that broken old car, with all sorts of things wrong with them. But God doesn't want us to stay like that. He wants us to find out what needs fixing and then bring it to Him for restoration.

To get the chassis of the car straightened, I first had to get a copy of the engineer's blueprint for the car, so that I would know exactly how it should be put together again. Our creator God has the "blueprint" for each one of our lives. He not only knows exactly what has happened to us over the years, but He also knows how we should be restored. So when He shows us what needs fixing, we can then set out on that wonderful journey of discovery with Him.

Weeding my Patch

I enjoy gardens, but I am no lover of the process of gardening. I am a completer-finisher by nature, and I don't like having to do a job again. Once it's done I like to move on to something else and not have to keep on doing the same thing over and over again. But all my experience of gardening tells me, that once the job has been done, it won't be long before it needs doing again! For weeds keep on growing – over and over again. And if you don't keep on top of the weeding they will take over the garden.

I love rhubarb. And once, in a fit of enthusiasm, I bought some rhubarb plants, prepared a patch of the garden to grow them in and planted them with great faith and expectancy. But such is the busyness of life that I didn't have the time to tend the rhubarb patch and before very long the nettles and other weeds had taken over, swamped the rhubarb and I was never able to enjoy the fruits of my original labors.

There was nothing wrong with the original rhubarb plants – they were good. It wasn't their fault that they were never able to deliver me a good crop. The fault was entirely mine. I'd failed to weed the patch and give the rhubarb plants a chance to grow. The weeds stole the water and nourishment from the ground, crowded out the light and, eventually, overran the ground.

This is a very accurate picture of what will happen to our Christian lives if we don't apply the principles of spiritual weeding to each area of our lives. Just as the land is opposed by the growth of weeds which appear to come from nowhere (Genesis 3:17) and grow big and strong without any effort, our lives are equally opposed by the temptations that come our way and the bad fruit that grows as a consequence of past sins and wounds.

In Jesus we have wonderful new life – but if we don't keep on weeding the patch of ground that our lives represent, that new life will be slowly choked by the competition coming from many other things. Jesus told a parable about the seed that fell on various types of ground. In one type of ground (see the story in Matthew 13) there are weeds and Jesus describes these as the bad growth that opposes fruitfulness in our lives.

So each of us has a job to do – to ask God to help us examine our life carefully so that we will recognize when various different weeds are growing there. We can either deal with the weeds ourselves or ask someone we know and trust to help us with tackling the problem and pray with us.

What are the Weeds?

There are three different types of weed that we need to look out for:

Firstly, the weeds which are a consequence of our own sins – the things we know are wrong but which we nevertheless do. Scripture is very clear that if we confess our sins (that means agree with what God thinks about them), then God will forgive us and cleanse us from all unrighteousness (1 John 1:9).

But James also says in James 5:16 that to be healed of the consequences of those sins we may need to confess them one to another – this deals with our pride and it is like pouring spiritual weed-killer onto the ground in which these weeds have grown.

Being forgiven by God, for what we have done wrong, and being healed of the consequences of those things are not necessarily the same thing – especially if a long time has passed between doing the sin and eventually confessing it. The passing of time gives weeds an opportunity to consolidate in our lives. Even physical conditions and illnesses can result from what we have done wrong.

I will never forget the lady who wanted prayer for a damaged neck from a car accident that took place sixteen years previously. When I prayed I didn't sense God was doing anything. I was then prompted to ask why she was in the car at the time of the accident. Her answer gave the key to why she was not being healed. There was a sin issue that had to be dealt with first for she was on her way to commit adultery at the time of the accident! She was being held in bondage by the enemy to the unconfessed sin of her past. It is only by bringing things into the light that the powers of darkness can be overcome.

On another occasion a lady came to a meeting wanting God's blessing on her life. But during the teaching, that came before the prayer ministry, I had been prompted by the Lord to say how important it is to conduct all our affairs with financial integrity. At the end of that teaching session the lady came and confessed to me that over many years she had stolen tens of thousands of pounds from her employers in small amounts of money one day at a time. No wonder she could not sense the blessings and presence of God in her life. There was a serious financial integrity issue standing between her and God.

So when it comes to producing good fruit for the Kingdom of God from the life God has given us, it is vital that we deal with the weeds that have grown up as a result of the wrong choices and outright sins we have committed, otherwise they will simply be a stronghold which the enemy can use to keep us under his control.

Secondly, there are the things that people have done to us. When we are hurt by others it causes pain. Pain is never pleas-ant, but if we choose not to forgive those who have hurt us the consequential damage is much greater than the initial pain that was suffered. The initial pain is caused by the things that are said or done to us at the time – the long-term damage is caused by the bitterness and unforgiveness in our hearts, as we learnt in Chapter 5.

If we deal with this as Jesus told us to, then even though there may be damage at the time, in the long term we will be free of the weeds that would otherwise grow up in our patch. Bitterness of heart is a rich feeding ground for the enemy. It's no surprise, therefore, that Jesus was so uncompromising over our need to forgive others for what they have done to us.

There can be many different people that we need to forgive, but perhaps the most significant are our parents. Whilst many people have been brought up by wonderful parents, this is not always the case. Increasingly, we are having to walk through the unique consequences of children having been brought up in one-parent families. God intended children to be brought up *"in the nurture of the Lord"* by a godly set of parents. The lack of fathering or mothering leaves a devastating hole in the emotions of a growing child.

It's not easy for people who have been very damaged as a result of their parenting to obey the fifth commandment which says, *"Honor your father and your mother."* The wonderful thing about this commandment is that it also contains a promise, *"so that you may live long in the land."* So how can you honor parents that have either deserted or abused you? The answer is simple – no matter how bad one's parents might have been, it is fact that they were God's vehicle of life for you. God used them to give you life. So we can always honor our parents for this one thing – and forgive them for everything they did which was ungodly.

This area of life's garden is often the most overgrown. It's no surprise, therefore, that giving some solid attention to weeding this patch will produce enormous fruit – even leading to significant physical healing.

Thirdly, there are the things we have inherited. Even though such things may be real, you may well be asking, *"What can I do about that?"* I once prayed with an unmarried lady called Mary Robinson. There were obvious characteristics about her behavior which were both ungodly and unpleasant for other people to have to live with. Whenever she was challenged about the contentious way in which she related with other people, she simply replied, "We Robinsons are always like that!" And that was probably the reason why she was yet unmarried.

Now that might have been her experience, but in reality it is not the whole truth. These particular Robinsons may have been bad-tempered, awkward people for many generations. But there's no reason why they should stay like that for generations to come. Another man said, "My grandfather committed adultery, my father committed adultery and now I've come here for help because I've committed adultery." He was holding the hand of his six-year-old boy at the time and, looking at him, asked me, "What hope is there for my son?"

Both these stories are typical of many family lines. There are behaviors of all sorts that get handed down from one generation to another, but it needn't be like that. There is an answer. But none of us can ever make the answer our own unless we face reality about ourselves. It is sometimes very hard to see ourselves as others see us. We have become so used to being the person we are, we automatically assume that how we are is how we are and evermore shall be so!

In order to comb our hair we need a mirror. And to look at our inner lives we need a human mirror to help us face reality about ourselves. With the help of others, who love us enough to be honest, we can then ask God to help us deal with those aspects of our lives where ungodliness has become the norm.

Forgiving our parents, grandparents, great-grandparents and even more distant ancestors is an important place to begin weeding this particular patch of our lives – forgive them for everything they have done which has given you a distorted view on life. In some cases there will be a spirit that needs to be dealt with – especially if there has been involvement in things like witchcraft, the occult, Freemasonry, false religions, ungodly sexual activities. The enemy will do everything he can to use these things to get demonic strong-holds in our lives and undermine our capacity to fulfill the destiny God has for each one of us.

Our Thought Life

Paul urges us as believers to *take every thought captive unto Him (2 Corinthians 10:5)*. And at the beginning of Romans 12 he says, *"be transformed by the renewing of your mind."* The reason is simple – everything we do in life begins as a thought.

The thought life is the source of all our words and actions. If we can learn to make Jesus Lord of our thought life, we'll have the keys to open every door in our life to Jesus. He'll be welcome in all the rooms of our house. We won't then be encouraging the growth of weeds in the garden of our lives by dwelling on ungodly thoughts.

It's worth remembering here that Jesus equated thoughts of adultery (lusting after a woman) to adultery itself. Something that is confirmed by Hebrews 4:12, where it says that God will judge the thoughts and intentions of the heart. This is very important for those who are overwhelmed by the temptation to escape into the unreality of sexual fantasies or, even, ungodly sexual relation-ships. It is vital that Jesus is Lord of our mind. If the battle is won in this area, then our behavior will be godly and the weeds will not be able to grow in the garden of our life.

Areas of Influence

In addition to weeding the patch of our inner lives, we next need to look at our areas of influence and responsibility. These also are *our patch.* Firstly there is our family and our home. God requires us to bring godly order *into* these. Godly order is realized by applying godly standards of truth, love and integrity to the way we live.

Our place of work is also our patch and if we bring godly order here it will not only be a blessing to those we work with but it will also ensure that the enemy doesn't have a back-door into our lives to control us. In fact, any area of responsibility that we have is under our personal authority and where we have personal authority we also have spiritual authority – both for good and bad.

The Fruit

A well-weeded garden will always be more fruitful than one that is left to run wild. Most significantly, the purer the vessel, the easier it is for us to hear the voice of the Lord as we seek to follow Him day by day.

Perhaps the greatest single key to fruitfulness is learning to listen to His voice so that we are constantly aware of His presence and able to respond gladly to His leading and direction. The more ungodly things there are in our lives the less easy it is to hear His voice. So regularly weeding your own patch is not just a chore, but an absolutely vital key to the effectiveness and fruitfulness of your Christian life.

Summary

A garden is only kept tidy by constant weeding. Our lives are only kept pure by constant attention to the detail – recognizing the ungodly and dealing with it appropriately and encouraging and developing the godly. If we do so we can confidently expect the fruit of the spirit to grow to maturity in our lives.

CHAPTER 11

FINDING MY DESTINY

The Beatles were one of many pop groups that changed the face of pop music for ever. Sadly, however, their unique and vibrant style was hijacked by the spirit of the age and, along with most such groups originating in the swinging sixties, moral and spiritual boundaries were ignored. And when the group became intimately involved in the new age and occult practices of Indian mysticism, a whole generation of young people across the world were introduced to a dangerous form of spirituality which has had a powerful deceptive influence on millions of people.

Of the four Beatles, two are still alive as I write. John Lennon was shot dead in New York. And George Harrison died of cancer. It is reported that shortly before he died he asked the following three very poignant questions:

Who am I?

What am I doing here?

Where am I going?

In the earlier chapters of this book, we have already looked at answers to the first and the last question. It is knowing who we are in God, and that our eternal destiny is secure in Him, that gives meaning and purpose to the second question – what am I doing here?

The need to be valued for who we are, and to have a purpose in life, is inbuilt into the spirit of every human being. This is part of our God-given identity. Life without a purpose is meaningless. One of the primary reasons why some people consider committing suicide is the apparent meaninglessness of their existence. Having lots of money and big houses will never satisfy the spiritual needs of the human being. It is not only poor people who think about taking their own lives. People from all strata of society, all ages and all levels of income can come to the same tragic conclusion.

Because we are at our core spiritual beings, mankind has always needed a form of spiritual fulfillment. That is why every people group ever researched by anthropologists has always had some form of worship at the heart of their culture. Man searches after the source of his life, after a Creator. Man needs to know his Creator and he also needs to know that we all have a purpose to live for – a destiny to fulfill.

Christians have believed and taught for two millennia that it is only when our spirits are anchored in God, through Jesus Christ (and all that means in terms of forgiveness of sin and restored relationship with God), that we can ever understand and know what it is God has created us for and answer George Harrison's question *What am I doing here?*

My Journey of Discovery

I was about nine years of age when I became a believing Christian. I clearly remember kneeling by my bedside, with my father kneeling beside me. Even though I was young, I was very much aware of the spiritual battle that was taking place that night. It seemed as though within me there was a huge resistance to praying the prayer which would transform every day of the rest of my life. But I desperately wanted to pray the prayer, because I knew that without Jesus my eternal destination would definitely not be heaven! Thankfully, I overcame that resistant inner voice and chose to invite Jesus into my life. I have never regretted the decision. It was the best decision I ever made.

Two things happened at that time – both of which I was very much aware of as the days, weeks and months passed. I knew for certain that my destination had changed and that heaven was now my eventual eternal home. But I also knew that my life now had a purpose beyond the obvious things that I enjoyed as a boy and would later enjoy as an adult, such as cricket, football, fishing and a hundred other exciting activities that filled the imagination of a post-war boy in northern England. The world was coming alive again after the Second World War and people talked excitedly about a new and safer world. It felt good to be alive.

I began to pray for God to show me what He wanted me to do and while there were a number of careers I could and would follow for a season, I could never shake out of my thinking the idea that one day I would be a preacher, or a pastor, or work in some sort of church-based activity.

If older people asked me the question that all kids hate, *"What are you going to be (or do) when you grow up?"* I would generally respond by saying "go into the church" or "be a minister," but only because I was connecting with what God must have planted deep into my spirit – even before I was born. Jeremiah 1:5 talks of Jeremiah's own origins when he says, *"Before I formed you in the womb I knew you, before you were born I set you apart, I appointed you as a prophet to the nations."*

As Jeremiah matured into a man of God, he obviously connected with what God had already spoken into his being. He was discovering what God had made him for – he was discovering his destiny.

The picture on the front of a packet of seeds is never of the seeds in the packet! I recently bought some runner bean seeds – only because my mouth began to water at the sight of the picture of freshly picked runner beans! I love them. The destiny of each seed in the packet was shown in the picture. It's a bit like that with God – He sees the destiny on the packet which contains the seed of our life. Little by little we become aware of what God has in store for our lives, as we grow in Him and mature as disciples of Jesus.

For twenty years I pursued careers in education and then the world of business as a publisher and bookseller. But throughout every one of those years the seeds of destiny were growing. I knew that what I was doing through those often difficult years was preparation for whatever God had made me for. It was my responsibility to remain faithful to God in my daily walk with Him while, at the same time, keeping my eye on the distant horizon looking for the fulfillment of destiny to come into view and then in to close-up focus.

Searching for Your Destiny

A believer who has chosen to live a godly life and become a disciple of Jesus Christ is now ready to enjoy the privilege of being used by God in His Kingdom purposes. It wasn't just Jeremiah that was known of God before he was born – each and every one of us was known by God in this way. He prepared for us the gifts and abilities appropriate for the destiny purpose God had in mind for our lives. We are all special and unique to Him. Psalm 139:13 tells how God created our inmost being and knit us together in our mother's womb.

God has had His hand upon us since those very earliest of days and has longed to see us, as His children, take the place in life for which He had prepared and equipped us. The joy that parents get when they see their children growing up into adulthood and maturity is simply a reflection of the greater joy that Father God experiences when He sees His children living in the reality of their destiny.

So, in learning to be a disciple, we are not only choosing to live a godly life, we are also being prepared to fulfill our destiny! As we put ourselves in the way of God, by our willing obedience to Him, we are creating the spiritual conditions for hearing His voice, giving us encouragement and direction for our lives.

Learning by Example

Learning to hear and respond to the voice of God is one of the most important lessons that a disciple can learn. My dad taught me that lesson from a very early age. No, he didn't take me aside and give me a lecture on how to hear the voice of God; I simply watched him day by day and learned from his example. He would read the Bible every day. He involved us children in his praying. It became just as natural to pray as to ask Mum to pass the butter at the tea table. I heard Mum and Dad pray together about problems – and I took note of the many, many times God answered their prayers, often in very remarkable ways.

And then there were the big decisions of life – such as career moves, changing jobs and moving house. Step by step Dad moved into his destiny. I learned the lesson that today's obedience lays the foundation for tomorrow's miracle! Mum supported him every inch of the way in his personal pilgrimage. I was learning vital lessons, without even knowing I was at school! No one told me that God has a destiny for my life; I just knew it, as I watched what was happening and learned about the faithfulness of God.

God rarely takes new believers and just drops them into their destiny. Few would be strong enough spiritually to withstand the pressures. It takes a moment for a couple to conceive a child – but it takes twenty years to grow a man or woman! In just the same way we can be born again in a moment of time, but it takes a period of years to grow a disciple of Jesus Christ who is ready to enter into their destiny. One of the greatest needs in the church today is for fathers in the faith to mentor the younger believers as they grow up into maturity. The greatest fruitfulness and greatest joy is ours, when we are doing those things that God has made us for and we fulfill our destiny purpose.

Satan – the Destiny Robber

Satan's ultimate objective is to receive the worship that is due to Almighty God. As we saw in the first chapters of this book, Satan began this process by tempting mankind to obey him and, in so doing, turn their eyes away from God and obey the one who became known as the god of this world – Satan became the object of man's worship.

When mankind continues to serve Satan and chooses to ignore the Savior who showed us the Way, the Truth and the Life, then the full destiny of a human being cannot be realized. It is only when all the gifts and abilities that God gave us in the first place can be brought into line with God's best for our lives that we can enter into the fullness of our destiny.

So, whilst there may be a battle to prevent a person choosing to become a Christian, once that battle has been won and lost (by the enemy), then Satan changes his tactic. He may have lost one battle but he then seeks to win the next battle – that is to prevent someone fulfilling their destiny purpose.

For when we are doing that which God made us for we are at our most effective as members of the Kingdom of God – both in bringing godly order into our personal and family lives, being powerful witnesses in our place of living and place of work and our lives being used in the best possible way to oppose the works of the enemy and build the Kingdom of God.

It is at this point that the healing ministry becomes a vital agent in the work of discipling believers. If a person breaks their leg and it doesn't set properly they will remain a cripple and be unhealed for the rest of their days. They will never be able to run again, climb a ladder or ride a bicycle. Their activities will be severely restricted because of the physical disability. They will be alive and may live a long life, but in the physical realm they will have had to be content to live within their physical limitations.

In much the same way, Satan seeks to use the restrictions of an unhealed past to hold us back from being and doing all that God intended. When we come to Jesus and receive Him as Savior and Lord, our sins are forgiven and our eternal destiny is secured. But Scripture makes it clear that we then have to work out our salvation (our healing!) with fear and trembling. And as we do so, we often find that physical healing is a side effect of the spiritual healing. Our bodies can be a reflector of what's going on inside, so that when God brings His order to the inside our physical well-being is changed as a result. We have seen conditions as varied as severe psychiatric symptoms and childlessness be healed as a result.

No wonder James said (James 5:16) that we should confess our sins one to another so that we may be healed. We also need to forgive those who have hurt us and to ask God to set us free from all the consequences of wrong things that have influenced our generation line. Often people need help with seeing the things that need to be done. As we saw in the last chapter, weeding the patch of our individual lives is essential!

God's Strategy for Your Destiny

Throughout Scripture and throughout history God led His people through relationship and by giving them His vision for their lives. God gave Noah a vision to build an ark. He gave David the vision of how to bring down Goliath. He gave Anna and Simeon a vision that one day they would welcome the Christ-child into the world and pronounce over Him when He was presented at the Temple.

Peter had a vision which meant that believing Jews should now take the gospel to the gentile peoples of the world. He gave Paul a vision to take the gospel into Europe when he saw in a dream a man calling out to him for help from Macedonia. And in more recent days He gave a young woman called Jackie Pullinger a vision for the drug addict society of the walled-city in Hong Kong.

Ephesians 1:5 talks about how, in love, God predestined us to be adopted as His sons – in other words He gave us a destiny in advance. God's fundamental desire for each one of us is that we should find first our eternal destiny in a restored relationship with God, and then begin to walk in our earthly destiny as citizens of the Kingdom of Heaven.

I was brought up with the story of two young women, Phoebe Lewsey and Ida Whittle, who loved the Lord and sensed the call of God for bringing hope and healing to the leper children of Northern Nigeria. I knew the story because Mum and Dad helped coordinate the support for their work. They allowed me to count the pennies in the missionary boxes and I really sensed I was doing my bit to help the missionaries. Involvement changes hearts and lives.

Phoebe and Ida gained encouragement from some UK Christians and they sailed in faith, with no knowledge or expectation of what they would find when they got there, and established the work of the *Albarka Fellowship* in Kaduna.

They were unknown to most of the Christian world, but in their faithfulness to the vision God had given them, they experienced extraordinary protection and provision, saved the lives of hundreds of children and knew personal miraculous healing from advanced cancer. One day there will be a roll-call in heaven of the lives that were transformed by the power of God through their ministry. Today many of those children are now serving the Lord in different parts of the world!

Scripture tells us that without vision people are perishing. Vision brings life and hope, purpose and destiny – both to ourselves and everyone whose life is touched by ours. It is important, therefore, that believers should really look to God to envision them for their lives. For when we are living out the visions that come from God we will know the greatest joy possible as we serve Him.

Vision is Not Enough!

Vision is essential, but one can have many visions sitting in an armchair and, without fail, none of them will be fulfilled – without the addition, that is, of two vital extra ingredients – faith and obedience.

Hebrews 11:6 tell us that without faith it is impossible to please God. It is faith that takes the barebones of a vision and begins to pray into how it might be fulfilled. A person of faith believes in the impossible and having carefully tested the vision before God, and with those whom you know and trust in God, starts to take action to put the vision into practice.

It is obedience which transforms a vision into the reality of destiny fulfilled! As I read the stories of the great pioneers I see in them all the moment when they left their "armchair" and, notwithstanding any opposition, set out to do what God had asked them to do and enter into their destiny.

The nature of vision varies from one person to the next, but God chooses those for particular opportunities that He has gifted and equipped them for. So a good place to begin the pilgrimage of destiny is to ask, *What do I enjoy doing?* And *What am I good at?* These will give you clues to your areas of gifting. You can then begin to pray and ask God to show you how He wants you to use those gifts and, yes, to give you His vision for your life.

I pray that as you walk this exciting walk of faith, God will clearly show you His best for the rest of your life and then, as you walk in faith and obedience to His vision, He will give you the joy of being fulfilled in the service of the King!

And it's Never Too Late for You!

Some of you reading this may be thinking that because the early days of your life were a long way from ideal or you have really got messed up along life's journey, for one of a variety of possible reasons, that you no longer have a realizable destiny or that God can no longer use you. If that is what you believe, you are believing a lie.

You may not be able to start life again at a young age, but God is the great redeemer. Not only did He redeem us from the consequences of our sins, but He redeems our lives from the pit. He is the one who can restore the years that the locust has eaten. He is the one that can take the humble offering of our lives, at whatever stage we come to that point of absolute surrender to Him, and build something precious in time that will last throughout eternity.

All God asks of us is our availability – He will then take whatever abilities we may have and multiply them in the service of the King.

Summary

Becoming a believer in Jesus Christ is the beginning of a journey of discovery – discovering the wonderful love and nature of God, discovering ourselves and discovering the destiny God has prepared for us. As we look to God for His direction for our lives and walk in the vision that comes from Him we will know the deepest joy known to man and we will discover, as did Nehemiah, that the joy of the Lord will be our strength.

CHAPTER 12

FELLOWSHIP IN THE CHURCH

The church is not a building. Yes, we generally call the buildings that Christians meet in for worship "churches," but the church in Scripture is never described as a building. The church is always a body of believers who have been called out from the Kingdom of darkness to live under the Lordship of Jesus Christ in the Kingdom of God.

The Greek word *ekklesia* describes what we call a church. It literally means the called out ones. It is within the *ekklesia*, the church, that people are brought to faith and discover worship. They are also discipled in the faith and cared for in the family of God. From childhood to maturity, as men and women of God, they are trained for service in both the church and the world. We even find that the early Church provided for them materially, as those with resources helped those with none.

The church is also a training organization, through which God intended His people to get to know Him better, as they are taught the truth of God's Word from the Scriptures and learn how to relate with Him in prayer. Additionally the church would look after the elderly, the widows and the orphans, care for the dying, bury the dead, comfort those who mourn and encourage the saints!

All of this adds up to an amazing catalogue of activities for the church to be involved in. The truth is that the church was intended by God to be a comprehensive spiritual and physical resource nurturing and providing for believers from the cradle to the grave. It was designed to be a fellowship which only exists because all the members are in a personal relationship with Jesus, the King. Because they each know and love Him, they also love each other.

Although this sounds like a highly organized operation, making exclusive provision for its members, it was never intended that the church would only be an inward-looking, self-interested club. Christians are servants of the King and citizens of the Kingdom of God and, as such, are under orders to be salt and light in the world. It was Jesus who said to His disciples, tell the people you meet that the Kingdom of God has come near them.

The church was always intended to be an organization whose members lived out their lives in the reality of the marketplace of life as we'll see in more detail in the next chapter. Yet the world is a harsh and alien spiritual environment. Believers would never be strong enough to live out their faith there if it wasn't for the constant encouragement, fellowship and discipling in the local church.

If you take a live coal out of a roaring fire it will soon go out. Fellowship is an essential ingredient for living the Christian life. If we ignore the need for each of us to be part of the active Body of Christ we will, in time, suffer the consequences of isolation. We'll miss out on the enormous benefit of learning about God, and how to live the Christian life from God's Word through the preaching and teaching ministry of the church.

The church today, in most places of the developed world, may not be the source of all the supporting services that the early Church aimed to provide. Yet it is the only source of the essential spiritual services that are at the heart of living the Christian life. Our social services may provide welfare for the young or care for the elderly, but they will never provide the teaching, personal ministry and prayer support which we all need for growth as believers.

Throughout history, however, it is Christians of every generation who have generally been the first to see the predicament of those in the world who are hurting and in need, and have sought to take action to respond to these needs. It was Christians who forced through changes in the law to abolish slavery. It was Christians who had compassion on the destitute and started one of the world's most famous social and spiritual welfare institutions, the Salvation Army. And many of the early medical pioneers were Christians who studied medicine because of their concern for the sick.

Many of the early hospitals had Christian foundations – as is often revealed by their very names. Many of those today at the forefront of feeding the hungry are Christians who are laying down their lives for those who have nothing. All of this is a primary love response to the people God has made.

Isaiah 58:6–9 describes the sort of "fasting" that blesses God – loosing the chains of injustice, setting the oppressed free, sharing one's food with the hungry, providing shelter for those who have none (caring for the orphans) and clothing the naked. God links the fulfillment of this God-given calling for His people with answers to our prayers for healing, the protection that comes from being covered by the glory of the Lord and knowing that our cries to God will be heard and answered. Jesus said very similar things when He said that if we feed the hungry and care for the sick, it is as if we are feeding and caring for Him (Matthew 25:40).

So the fellowship of the church was intended by God to be an all-embracing resource for God's people financed by the giving of its members. It's intended to be a means of evangelism reaching out to those who do not know God. And it's the place in which people are trained as disciples of Jesus Christ.

Sadly, many churches believe their evangelistic responsibility to a person finishes when that person becomes a Christian. In reality that's the moment when the process of discipling believers, inside the fellowship of the church, should begin. Jesus did not tell the Church to go out into all the world and make believers, He told them to go and make disciples. God gives the new life through which a person is born again and becomes a believer. But it's the existing disciples who were commissioned by God to make disciples out of believers in every generation of church history.

How the Church is Run

Jesus is the head of the Church – often referred to as the Body of Christ (Colossians 1:18). It is called the Body of Christ because it is the organization that Jesus left behind to continue to do the work He started when He walked this earth. People saw Jesus, they heard Him teach as well as heal and deliver people. He fulfilled the prophetic vision of Isaiah 61:1 and healed the broken-hearted and set the captives free.

After Jesus went back to heaven, it was God's intention that people would then come to know Him through the Body of Christ. The church was to do the same things that Jesus had done – proclaim the Kingdom of God, heal the sick and cast out demons. And in order to do that, organization was needed. Jesus only had twelve disciples, perhaps indicating that this was as many as can be successfully trained in a small group. Anything bigger than this would need greater organization and structure. Growth was essential to cope with both the internal needs of the fellowship and the outward-facing needs of evangelism.

In Acts 6 the Apostles started this process by setting apart seven men to help with the organization. The basic qualification for being considered for the role was to be filled with the Holy Spirit – not ability or gifting. These men were to take on some of the management problems of distributing food to the hungry. As needs grew, so more organization became essential and the embryonic church began to take on a structure.

This episode in the growth of the Church highlights the fact that if we elevate gifting above godliness, and put people in places of authority for which they are not spiritually equipped, then we create problems for the Body of Christ. It can mean that we give the enemy an opportunity to control the church from within.

This has been a constant problem in every era of the Church and it is one of the main reasons why so much of organized church has become dysfunctional without spiritual authority. The inevitable consequence of this is either spiritual deadness or deception in the church – for without the fullness of the Holy Spirit there can be no exercise of the gift of discernment which is essential for identifying and eliminating those things that are not of God.

The developing church needed further organization and, at a later date, Paul taught how the Body of Christ was intended by God to be like a living, visible organism. It has different organs fulfilling different primary roles for the good of the whole.

In Ephesians 4:11 Paul identified different categories of leader. Some would be apostles, some prophets, and others evangelists, pastors or teachers. These are the five-fold giftings necessary for the effective running of the church so that it can fulfill God's destiny for the Body of Christ. And just as these categories of leadership were necessary in Paul's day, they are equally necessary today and need to be represented in the life of the denominational and local church. Paul was not giving teaching that was only relevant for the emergent church, he was laying down the foundations for the Body of Christ for the whole of time.

The apostles are those who are the visionary leaders. They hear the voice of God for the fellowship and its work. They see a long way ahead of everyone else and set out to take the people of God to the place God has shown. The prophets are those who are especially sensitive to hearing the heart of God. They bring correction as and when needed and share things that God might be saying to the leaders and the people as they follow the direction and lead of those with the apostolic gifting.

The evangelists are those with a special gifting to share the gospel with those who do not yet know Jesus. The pastors are those who have a heart of compassion for people and who can understand the needs of the people. They have a ministry of care, healing and deliverance. Finally the teachers are those with a special gift in being able to understand the Scriptures and communicate the heart of God to others so that they can learn the foundational truths of God's Word.

All of these, apostles, prophets, evangelists, pastors and teachers, may preach and teach the fellowship about the things they are especially gifted at. I don't think it was ever intended that only one person should carry the responsibility for all the preaching and teaching in the church. When that happens, it can have the effect of putting a bias on the nature of a particular congregation. For example, a congregation could be so focused on evangelism (because their minister is an evangelist by heart), that the congregation only ever hear the gospel message and never grow to maturity through the wider teaching of the Word of God.

Small Groups

The very first small group had Jesus as its group leader! Once they had been called out from their employment, they became the full-time support team for Jesus. They were also the embryonic church leadership group in training. It was in this precious nurturing environment that the foundations for the future Church were being laid down, even though I'm sure the disciples did not fully understand this until the end of their time of training, just before Jesus ascended back to heaven.

The small group is the place where fellowship is at its most intimate and valuable. It is here that people can study the Bible together, talk about important issues of Christian life and conduct, ask questions, discuss the answers, learn how to pray and support each other in whatever needs they may have.

The largest churches in the world today – some with many thousands of members in Brazil or Korea, for example – are organized into hundreds of small groups and this becomes the primary means of training disciples. Then when they come together with other small groups on a Sunday or at midweek services they can enjoy the richness of exciting corporate worship with hundreds, and even thousands, of other believers and absorb the teaching from the leaders in the main services and events of the organization.

Small groups are also an excellent place for people to develop their own giftings in a secure and safe environment. Potential leaders can be identified and given further training and little by little believers who came into the group as new Christians take major steps forward in their training as disciples – exactly what Jesus commissioned the Church to do. A church fellowship without a small group structure will generally lose touch with new believers, who may then fall away through lack of support and encouragement.

It is often in the small group situation that God begins to speak to individuals about their own calling in God as they seek to discover their destiny. It was in small group situations that God developed my own interest in helping people in need. People are much more relaxed about sharing the intimacies of their life in a safe environment with friends you know and who love you. Whenever this happened, something inside me always came alive and I would instinctively want to find out what I could do to help. I was learning about the healing and discipling ministries without even knowing what was happening.

Others developed their musical gifts. The group always spent time in worship at the beginning of each meeting. People who could only pluck a few chords on their guitar or play a few notes on the keyboard were motivated to learn more, practice and become quite accomplished. People with little confidence in themselves discovered that they, too, had gifts and abilities which were valuable and useful to others – that, in itself, is a major healing step for some people.

If people were absent from the group, it was a simple pastoral job to find out if they were OK and if there were any special needs. A congregation of twelve is easy to manage – but what precious times those days can be as people discover the joy of serving God by helping each other and being God's agent of love for someone else.

From time to time people would go through tough times – redundancy, financial hardship, relationship breakdown, betrayal, sickness, crises with the children were all issues that would surface in the group. Helping with things that would never normally surface in the congregation of a large church, became the bread and butter of small group fellowship. Lasting and even life-long relationships were made, providing a solid supporting network of friendships for the years that would follow.

It was Derek Prince who said, "If you want to be a leader, first learn to be a servant." There are many great leaders today who learned to serve in small groups and later became men and women of God with much wider ministries and influence in the Body of Christ.

Life-long Friendships

I've often talked in this book about the influence on me of my parents' Christian faith and life. It's not long since my mother went to be with the Lord. My father died many years ago. As the news of my mother's death spread among the circle of friends Mum and Dad had accumulated, in the different parts of the country they had lived and worshiped in, hundreds of cards and letters began to arrive.

I was seriously impacted by all the kind things that people said about both Mum and Dad. I appreciated, in a way that I had never fully appreciated before, how deep and precious and long-lasting is Christian fellowship and Christian relationships. Friendships that had spanned sixty and more years, many of which had continued with children and children's children were commonplace.

Many gave testimony and thanks for being introduced to Jesus and becoming Christians as a result of their friendship and encouragement. There were many who had been friends in the local church in their twenties and thirties – people they had prayed with, worshiped with, done beach missions with at Blackpool, Morecambe and in Northern Ireland. I caught just a tiny glimpse of what heaven is going to be like as we rejoice for eternity in the love and fellowship of those who love the Lord and love each other in Him!

Never underestimate how precious Christian fellowship is. There have been times in my own life when work has taken me into situations and environments where I have had little or no Christian fellowship. These have often been difficult times. It has always been a joy in such situations to discover a fellow-Christian and be blessed by the one-ness Christians have in their relationship with each other because of their individual relationships with Jesus. Occasionally I have the blessing on a flight of sitting next to a fellow Christian. It always amazes me how quickly one can establish precious fellowship and unity in Christ.

Summary

Fellowship is at the heart of growth to Christian maturity. It is seeing how God works in other people's lives that can often give us life-changing lessons. And at the same time we can receive the support that will equip us for life's journey. God intended the local church to be that safe place where we can build precious friendships and relationships. If we ignore the need for fellowship we will become islands without relationship and miss the very best that God intended for each and every one of us.

CHAPTER 13

MY LIFE IS NOT MY OWN – THE KEY TO GIVING

The Key to Giving

As long as man has been on the earth, giving has been part of both the worship of God and a source of blessing in human relationships. True giving to others is an expression of love between the giver and the receiver. The most extraordinary gift that has ever been given was the gift of Jesus, the Son of God, as an expression of love from Father God to the human race. As John 3:16 expresses it so powerfully, *"For God so loved the world that he **gave** his one and only Son, that whoever believes in him shall not perish but have eternal life"* (emphasis added). Giving, therefore, originated in the heart of God and was supremely expressed by His extraordinary act of love.

We are made in the image and likeness of God. It's no surprise, therefore, that giving to others as an act of love is not just something which Christians do; it's a universal love language of the human race! The act of giving says that I'm willing to sacrifice something that belongs to me so that I can bless you. Selfless giving always builds relationships.

When someone has a birthday, relatives and close friends will give a present. When you're invited round to someone's house for a meal, it's customary to take a gift with you as a way of saying thank you to your host. Couples in love will constantly be thinking of things they can give to each other as an expression of their love.

People celebrate their wedding anniversaries by giving love gifts to each other. And when an official delegation from one country makes a visit to see the head of State of another country, such as the Queen or the President, then it is customary to present an appropriate and significant gift. Giving is part of the expression of all levels of human relationship. And it originated in the heart of God!

Giving to God

Of course it's not possible for us to give physical gifts to God as He's a spiritual being, but we can give our hearts and lives to Him in response to His love. Instead of giving physical gifts to God, as an expression of our love, we can give them to others. In doing this we bless God. He made provision for this as part of the covenantal relationship between Himself and us.

Because man had sinned and couldn't think clearly about spiritual matters for himself, he needed guidance for how to live within the provisions of God's original plan for mankind. So it was required of God's people that a tithe (a tenth) of all their income, in both cash and kind, was expected to be given for the use of those who couldn't earn an income for themselves, because their lives were set aside to serve God's people in a priestly role. So the priests were supported by the faithful giving of the people.

The equivalent of this today would be the local church, so that the fellowship would have the funds to both pay a living salary to the pastor, other employed members of the church team and to pay the costs of upkeep of the buildings used by the fellowship for the work of the church.

This principle of giving a tithe was not built into the Ten Commandments, but was part of the additional rules and regulations for the people of God, until the time when the Old Covenant would be fulfilled with the coming of Jesus. When that time came, and God was able to write His law of love on the hearts of His people with the coming of His Spirit at Pentecost, people would then be able to choose to give, both to the running of church and in response to the needs of others, as an expression of their love of God, without the need for the amount to be laid down by a ten per cent rule.

The fundamental principle that pervades the whole of Scripture is not that we own what we have and give back to God a tenth of what is ours, but that everything belongs to God in the first place and we are privileged to be blessed by what He has provided! So we should always look on whatever we have been privileged to own as an entrustment from God to use for whatever purpose the Lord shows. But in the background we have that guidance from the Old Covenant. We should look on a tithe of our income as being that part which should be set aside for supporting the organization we call Church that God has set in place to support us throughout our lives.

There are many Christians today who still use the tithe as a basic guide to their minimum level of giving, to ensure that they keep in line with God's strategy for His people. It's so easy to put giving to others to the bottom of the list of commitments and making a discipline of being faithful in our giving will certainly bring God's blessing into our lives.

Heart Motive

I believe many people have misunderstood the Bible's teaching on giving and have fallen into the trap of giving with a wrong motive. They read Scriptures, such as Malachi 3:10–12, which encourage people to give their full tithe and talk about the wonderful, even extravagant, blessings that God will pour on their lives as a result.

The temptation is to think "I want to get blessed" so, in order to get blessed, people then give. But that way of thinking is a distortion of the truth of the Word of God and is sometimes referred to today as the prosperity gospel. The message people get is that if I want to be prosperous I must give as much as I can to the Church. The result of this can be that the Church becomes wealthy at the expense of the poor.

No, we should never give in order to get rich or to be blessed. The only right motive for giving is ultimately love – and we choose to be obedient to God in respect of our giving because we love Him, not because of the hope of a good return on our investment in God's work!

There is no doubt that if we are faithful in our giving, even when the cost of giving may be high, the time will come when God blesses us abundantly. But if we think that we will always see the blessing in this life, then we are being a little short-sighted. Paul often talks of the treasure that is laid up for us in heaven. Jesus talks about the place He's going to prepare for us. There is a reward laid up for those who truly love the Lord – and if we truly love Him, then we will gladly want to give of all that He has given us so that both God and others will be blessed by the sacrifices of our lives.

There's no certainty that as believers we will be exempt from all the difficulties of life that can come to both Christians and unbelievers. In 2 Corinthians 11:22–29 Paul lists many of the things that he has had to endure as an Apostle of Jesus Christ – including, the hallmarks of poverty, being without food and clothing.

God has promised to be with us at all times. But the Bible does not promise that we will always escape the problems of life. Many times I have had to pray with believers who have gone through really tough times and suffered many things. If their belief in God was such that they expected to escape all this sort of thing and enjoy unending prosperity, then the moment things didn't turn out as they wanted or expected, their faith in God would be shattered. I passionately believe in God and that God also heals, but unless we have a doctrine of suffering as well, compatible with the reality of the fallen world we live in, then we are living in unreality.

Practical Guidelines for Christian Giving

Returning now to our love response to God as the basis for our Christian giving, here are some practical principles to help you make godly choices about how you can use your resources to give responsibly to others:

1. Recognize that everything we own is ultimately a gift from God.

2. All our giving should be as a love response and thanksgiving to God and not be considered to be a means of trying to bribe God to bless us!

3. As people of the New Covenant, aware of the presence of God in each of our lives, we need to be asking God at all times to show us how to use the resources He's given us – not only our financial income, but our homes and our possessions as well.

4. Under the Old Covenant God gave His people a base-line guide for giving. The tithe was intended to be used to support the work and the ministry of the priests – not be the sum total of all giving. And we should recognize our responsibility to be giving to and through our local church so that the fellowship that supports us will not be lacking

in the funds they need to do the works of the Kingdom of God.

5. The Old Covenant tithe is not meant to be a legalistic requirement for Christians (New Covenant believers) – but if our overall giving is less than ten per cent, then there are some things out of balance in the way we conduct our finances that will need correcting.

6. We should always give freely and without strings. It is our responsibility to give. It's the responsibility of those to whom the gift has been given to use it wisely.

7. Finally, it's always good to pray for those people and organizations to which God calls us to give. When we give we are investing something of ourselves in the causes we give to and to follow this up with prayer and intercession is one way of contributing to the effectiveness of the work our gifts are supporting.

Many thousands of Christians can give testimony to the fact that when they have chosen to be obedient to what they have sensed God is telling them to give, and given generously with a thankful heart, they have discovered that God is no man's debtor. They have found the promise of 1 Samuel 2:30, *"Those who honour me, I will honour"* to be totally true. God has subsequently blessed and honored them – often in some very surprising ways.

What we give doesn't have to be big for it to be blessed. Jesus told a story of the woman who gave a very, very small sum – but it was all she had. It was, therefore, everything. Her commendation was far greater than a rich man would have received for a large gift, which he could easily afford. No wonder Jesus also told the sad story of the rich young ruler, whose riches had become an obstacle to his relationship with God. Jesus told him to go and give it all away!

So, ultimately, the key to giving is simply obedience. I love what happened at the wedding feast when they ran out of wine. Mary, the Mother of Jesus, simply told the servants to do whatever He tells you to do! (John 2:5). And that must be the key to giving for each one of us.

There will be times when God makes us very aware of somebody or something He wants us to give to. We can either say "yes" and do what God is saying – or miss out on God's chosen means to bless others through us. There have been a number of times in my own life when I have sensed God asking me to give – often at times when it seemed as though I could least afford it. But I have never regretted doing what God asked. God always blesses a generous heart. Sometimes we are privileged to share in the joy that our giving has released – and what a blessing that can be!

We need to value whatever God has entrusted to us, but hold it lightly, so that whenever He calls us to be generous we can give with a thankful heart and trust Him with the outcome.

Summary

If we are living a godly life, then we will have a desire to walk in the ways of God. He gave what was most precious to Him when He gave His Son. It's important that we learn to give joyfully to others as an expression of our love for God. He will always bless that which is given in love and obedience to Him.

CHAPTER 14

LIVING THE LIFE
IN THE MARKETPLACE

All One Life!

People sometimes talk of their Christian life as if it is a different life from the one of their work and play. The "sacred" and the "secular" can get divided from each other as if they should never be mixed. But in reality we only have one life to live and we live it in all sorts of different environments.

The Hebraic view of life is very different from our modern western culture. God is embraced as being included in every single aspect of life. The idea of sacred and secular does not exist in Hebraic thinking – all life comes from God and all of life belongs to God. Wherever I am and whatever I'm doing – it's all the life God has given me.

As we read the first eleven verses of Deuteronomy 28, we find that all the many different aspects of life – home, family, work and business – are of equal interest and importance to God and to those who are seeking to serve Him. The promises of God's blessing to those who keep God's covenant relate to every area of life – and not just what we might call the spiritual bits. In the later verses of this chapter we see that when God's people

ignore God's Word and God's law and disobey God's commandments, then every area of their life is affected. Everything from
health to family to business suffers when they move out from the
provisions God made for His blessing to be on them.

The Christian life is not just a life that's to be lived within
the confines of church. It's a life that's to have the source of its
strength in that church – but which is to be lived in the reality of
every aspect of our human existence.

So What is the Marketplace?

In recent years a new expression has entered the language of
Christian culture – "marketplace ministries." It is not, however,
a new concept, for the Church was founded in the marketplace
of life. Almost all the events recorded in the Acts of the Apostles
took place in the marketplace – the places of business, social and
recreational interchange.

For many years the method of most church-based evangelism has been to invite the unbeliever onto church turf – either
to meetings in a church building, or to a meeting organized by
church people in a specially rented auditorium or stadium. There
will always be a place for events such as this, but in recent years
there has been a sense that the season is changing. Today it's
more important to focus on making Jesus real in the ordinary
everyday environment in which people live and work – the
marketplaces of life. Church meetings are such a foreign environment for the majority of the unbelieving population that we must
learn new ways of meeting people on their territory rather than
just inviting them onto ours.

When Jesus sent the disciples out to proclaim the Kingdom of
God, He told them to say to the people that *"The kingdom of God
has come near to you"* (Luke 10:9, NASB). This was a dynamic new
concept for the disciples, for a Kingdom is ruled over by a King,
and a King has authority. So Jesus was telling His disciples that

wherever they went they could operate in the authority of the King – the authority Jesus Himself had given them.

So, with this authority in their armory, Jesus sent them out to proclaim the Kingdom of God, heal the sick and cast out demons. They came back excited and rejoicing at what they could now do. They had been into the marketplace with the teaching and ministry that Jesus had given them. They discovered that wherever they went, the God who had invited His people to come and worship Him in the Temple under the Old Covenant, was now going with them out into the highways and byways of life. They brought back stories of all the wonderful things that had happened in the marketplace! (Luke 10:17).

The marketplace is wherever we happen to be when going about the normal, everyday activities of our lives. The marketplace will be different for all of us. There are nine major arenas of the marketplace – all of which are part of the great marketplace of human experience and interchange. These are: education; science and technology; health care and social welfare; business; finance; government; law and law enforcement; communications and transport; media and entertainment. These are the places where people work and wherever believers work in these environments, the Kingdom of God is also there. It is there that we can do the works of the Kingdom as well as in the life of our local church fellowship.

Evangelism in the Marketplace

You will probably be thinking, "I'm not an evangelist," so what has this to do with *Living Life God's Way?* That's a perfectly good and fair question. But when you ask a large crowd of Christians what was the most significant factor in their own life story which influenced them in their decision to become a Christian, you will invariably discover that well over 50 per cent of the people will say something like the influence of a friend or colleague at work. Only a relatively small number refer to the influence of a particular evangelist. It is the living witness of Christian friends and family that's the most powerful and effective means of sharing the gospel with unbelievers.

It's a fact that perhaps 95 per cent of the people we meet in our particular marketplace arena will never come near a church. But, it's also a fact that close to a 100 per cent of the people, in every arena of life, will come face to face with a member of the Body of Christ on a regular basis.

So whether we consider ourselves to be evangelists or not, the fact is, we are – for, just as Jesus told the disciples, wherever we go, that's where the Kingdom is. Through all the contacts we make in our own marketplace arena we have endless opportunities to live a humble life of uncompromising Christian integrity and to use whatever opportunities the Lord gives us to share a word in season. Who we are and how we conduct our lives will be noticed by others. So often it's the impact of a life of godly integrity which has great significance in influencing the lives of others.

We don't have to think that it's our job to be the harvester of every soul we meet. But it is our job to be a link in the chain of truth that God seeks to forge in a person's life, so that they can consider for themselves the facts of the gospel. For me, personally, such instances range from praying for a man with a bad back, who had to unload a truck, to finding common ground with the passenger next to me on an airline flight and praying for the opportunity to relate something in our conversation to the Christian message. It's easier than you might think to build such a bridge into a person's life.

When in business, I built up a good relationship with my chief supplier. It wasn't very long before our conversations would turn to more than the business in hand. And eventually the day came when my business office became a marketplace church as my friend entered the Kingdom of God.

I know a successful stockbroker who employs several hundred people. Most of his non-Christian staff would never go to a church on a Sunday, so he runs a marketplace church on his business premises at lunchtime once a week. The Christian staff meet regularly to pray for the business and the employees. This has had a major impact on the business as more and more of the staff have become Christians.

One of the greatest missionary pioneers of all time opened up India for the gospel. But for the ten years before going to India, William Carey was a village shoemaker near Northampton and he would say, "My business in life is the salvation of souls and I cobble shoes to pay expenses." Whatever our marketplace arena might be (Carey's would have been in the retail/manufacturing sector of the business arena) we can have a similar attitude. Our spiritual business in life is to live so that our lives fulfill our Kingdom destiny in God and so that we're always a dynamic and living witness to our faith. It's our work in the marketplace that provides the income to pay the expenses of living.

When Work Challenges Faith

Mixing the world of work and the walk of faith is not always easy, especially when there are issues of integrity or morality at stake. There have been a number of times recently in the public arena where a person's Christian rights have been challenged by their employer – even on some occasions finishing up in high-profile court cases with varying outcomes, some successful and others unsuccessful.

The situation also varies greatly from country to country where different governmental authorities and local religions can have a huge effect on the attitude to Christian faith and practice. It was relatively easy in the UK, until the British rule of law parted company from the ethics and morality of traditional Christian beliefs. But now we live in a different world where people from all faiths and consequential beliefs are accorded equal rights and sexual ethics and morality are no longer considered to be relevant issues for consideration in modern society.

Christians have no problem with loving all people, irrespective of their faith, sexual orientation or morality. We serve a God who IS love and we, therefore, are also motivated by the same depth of love for all humanity. But there's a huge difference between loving all humanity and being obliged to approve of what others do or believe. Even worse than that would be the prospect of Christians having to become participants in things they consider ungodly or, to put it in scriptural terms, things they consider sinful. There is no doubt that God loves all men, but there is equally no doubt from Scripture at the grief and pain caused to the heart of God when those He loves behave in a way that's contrary to His nature and character.

The area of finances and business ethics is also a potential minefield – especially if an employer is asking an employee to do something which is either illegal or immoral. For example, such things as accepting cash payments and not putting them through the company books as a means of tax evasion is illegal in most, and probably all, government regimes. But it's not uncommon for a person's job to be under threat if they don't participate in this or similar practices which are technically illegal, but which are commonly encountered. Employers will sometimes ask their staff to tell lies on their behalf in order to cover up something in the company, or to win a sales contract by promising a delivery date which they know cannot be achieved.

How are Christians meant to respond in such situations? For me, personally, there can only be one guiding principal and that is humility and respect towards one's employers, but the exercise of truthfulness at all times. There may be occasions when taking such a stand may be very costly, even resulting in the loss of a job – but surely it is better to lose a job than to compromise one's relationship with God?

Spiritual Authority in the Marketplace

Land, organizations and businesses can all be spiritually affected by what has happened there previously. This is because, in the first place, God gave authority over the earth to mankind. It's interesting that in Genesis 4, after the murder of Abel by Cain, Scripture tells us how his blood cried out to God from the ground. The ground itself had been affected by what Cain had done.

Just as we can sense the blessing of God's Spirit in a place that has been set aside for godly purposes, it's also true that where there has been ungodliness practiced, of whatever nature, the enemy has been given a right there by sinful behavior. Unless we deal with that spiritual authority, then we will be influenced by it.

For example, I have prayed with many people over the years who have come under the influence of a sexual spirit in such circumstances and have not understood why they suddenly felt vulnerable to sexual temptations. That's why we train our teams to always exercise their spiritual authority in hotel bedrooms and cleanse the room before taking up occupancy. Hotel rooms are a favorite place for people to watch pornography or have an illicit sexual relationship and leave behind an atmosphere of spiritual uncleanness.

Legal authority and spiritual authority go hand in hand. Wherever a person has rightful legal authority they also have the right to exercise their own spiritual authority in that place. So an occupant of a hotel bedroom, an employee of a company or a teacher in a classroom has the spiritual authority before God to pray in that room and cleanse it of ungodly spiritual influence left behind by previous occupants or anyone who once held responsibility there.

To establish your own godly authority in this way prepares the ground for more effective and fruitful work. It's not unusual for people to come into an office that has been cleansed in this way and comment on how nice the office feels – even visitors can sometimes sense it.

There is no need to be overly religious about the process of cleansing. It's enough to pray a simple prayer of binding any spirit that has had rights there and then exercise your spiritual authority in Jesus to prevent it from ever influencing you and ordering it out of the domain in which you have legal authority. This will transform the spiritual environment in which you are working. I would also then simply consecrate the place of work – be it just one desk or a whole office – and offer yourself afresh to God to serve Him in this place of employment in your personal marketplace.

You can also discreetly anoint the place with oil declaring it now to be holy ground (see Exodus 40:9 for a scriptural example of the principle). The transformation in the working environment that can result from exercising such simple spiritual authority often surprises people. The marketplace is where we live and work. Why not ensure that the place where you spend such a large amount of your time is as clean as possible for your time of service there?

Kingdom Businesses

One of the most interesting aspects of Christian life today is a resurgence in what are generally called *Kingdom Businesses* – businesses which have been established by Christians, to be run with the utmost of integrity as a means of both interfacing with the unbelieving world and providing employment for Christians in the local community which does not present them with moral dilemmas.

One church I know in Eastern Europe adopted this as a policy, instead of following the line of many other such churches who continued to rely on donation income from the "wealthy west." The church leaders established a number of successful businesses in the town. These provided income for the church and employment for the community. As a result they enjoyed the blessings of God on their endeavors in line with the promises of Deuteronomy 28:1–11. Instead of being a church which was dependent on outside support, they themselves became a church which was pioneering evangelism in other areas using the resources they were generating through business.

Another pioneering church in the UK adopted a similar policy and has built a series of Kingdom businesses, in areas as varied as double-glazing and media design. These have been fundamental to the remarkable growth of the church and its influence in the town and community they serve. Instead of asking their local authority for funding, they have been able to go to the local authority to ask how they may help serve the community better.

This is primary evangelism which prompts people to ask real questions about why Christians are doing such things. The problem with much traditional evangelism is that the evangelists are answering questions that no one is asking! It's only when people ask their own questions, as a result of their experience of meeting and working with Christians, that we are able to speak with authority into their lives with answers that are relevant to where they're at.

I know also of two groups of people who have been faced with the huge ethical problems which can be associated with the world of finance and banking. So they have taken action to resolve the situation and founded their own Christian banks! Clearly this is something that only a very few people can consider, but it is indicative of a major move that is currently changing the way churches think about their role in the local community.

In the nineteenth century there were some very big companies started by Christian entrepreneurs with a desire to provide secure employment and good working conditions. They developed businesses, built housing for the workers, paid them a fair wage and saw God bless their endeavors. Some of these companies went on to be the major business players of the twentieth century.

It seems as though we are now going through a major renaissance in the development of Christian businesses, with many large churches, especially in North America, encouraging their young people to start and develop Kingdom businesses with the prayer and support of the church behind them.

Summary

The marketplace is where most Christians live out the largest proportion of their waking time. It's a vital place of Christian witness and service, providing many opportunities for sharing one's faith with others. In the case of Kingdom businesses, it provides opportunities for Christians to interface with the world as well as fulfill their destiny in a Christian environment in a God-honoring way.

CHAPTER 15

RECREATION

God's Plan from the Beginning

God's plan for the human race included provision for rest and recreation right from the very beginning. On the seventh day of creation God rested and in so doing set an example for man because He knew that man would need to rest. When God gave to Moses the Ten Commandments, each of them written in stone by the finger of God, the Sabbath rest principle was also part of these vital foundations for life. God didn't intend that these commandments should ever fall into disuse – they were written in stone!

The Sabbath Rest

If land is used year in and year out without ever giving it a rest, then the productivity quickly declines and the harvest gets less year after year. If the land is allowed to lie fallow one year in seven, it recovers itself and is fit for another six years of productive harvesting. This principle of rest and recovery is built into the life-cycle of humanity, as well as being the means through which God provides for the ongoing provision of food for human beings. In the Christian era Sunday was adopted as the day of rest instead of the Jewish Sabbath (Saturday), but the principle remains the same.

This Judeo-Christian principle became the normal practice for many centuries in all countries where Christian principles provided the foundation for life and government. In the 1940s and 1950s, the days of my own childhood, you wouldn't be able to find a shop open on a Sunday and public transport was severely limited. Virtually no one worked on a Sunday. Most of the nation closed down from Saturday night till Monday morning.

As a reaction against this Christian ethos, some of the early communist societies decided to abandon the Sunday principle in an attempt to increase productivity. They made every day the same and abandoned the idea of a day of rest. They were expecting a significant increase in production, with an extra day's useful work having been completed. It wasn't long, however, before they discovered, much to their surprise, that productivity fell! The workforce was incapable of sustaining the pressure of continuous work and they had to reinstate a rest day, in line with God's best plan for the human race, in order to maintain productivity.

Most nations now work a five-day week, providing ample time for both rest and recreation, so the next question to ask is, "How should we use the rest and recreation time we have available?"

God had two objectives for His people in providing a Sabbath day's rest for them. One was to give their whole being – spirit, soul and body – time to rest and recover from the labors of the week that had passed. The second was to ensure that God's people had time to nurture their relationship with God through worship and being taught by those God had put in place as their teachers.

So, as part of the synagogue worship of His day, Jesus, as a rabbi, was a regular speaker at synagogue services, in much the same way as Christian pastors today would preach and teach when their people come together to worship God. In Luke 4:16–21 Jesus used just such an opportunity to declare His own personal mission statement, as He taught from Isaiah 61:1–2.

Worship must be a vital part of our lives as God's people today, just as it was in the days of the Old Covenant up to the time Jesus came. The Psalmist expresses the reason for this very clearly when he says that God inhabits the praises of his people (Psalm 22:3). The word "inhabit" means "come inside to dwell." So worship provides the means through which God indwells His people and His people renew their fellowship and relationship with their God.

It's not that God can't exist without His creation adoring and worshiping Him. It's simply that God is our Creator, and He knows how much we need a relationship with Him. We worship Him because of who He is and through that act of submission to our Creator, we are strengthened to continue fulfilling our destiny. We live and move and have our being in Him. Time to focus on who God is and our relationship with Him is a vital part of being human. We bless God through our worship and He indwells our lives as we worship.

Being in the fellowship of God's people in our local church is an important expression of regular worship. These regular times are vital to our growth as Christians. We can worship God together, receive good teaching and share in different aspects of serving Him through the activities of the fellowship we belong to. We mustn't make the mistake, however, of only worshiping God on that one day in seven. The Hebraic understanding of worship draws on the reality that we are God's children twenty-four hours a day and seven days a week and that at all times we need to be aware of the presence of God.

Whenever I see something beautiful in His creation I turn what I'm seeing into an act of worship of the Creator. It's not hard to praise Him when your eyes and ears are open. I'm writing this chapter close to an amazing beach on the western shores of Scotland. As I hear the waves crashing on the shore, see the outstretched sand being washed clean twice a day by the tides and experience the glorious setting sun paint an extraordinary picture on the western horizon, my heart is filled with joy and thanksgiving for this incredible world He made for us.

Psalm 19 expresses this so well when the Psalmist says that nobody in the world can fail to understand the message God is constantly giving to human beings, as they observe the sun, the moon, the stars and all created realms. Our God is a great and mighty God – He is worthy to be praised.

In Jesus' day some of the Pharisees had seriously misunderstood the purpose of the Sabbath and had a whole series of inappropriate rules and regulations about what one can and cannot do on the Sabbath. Orthodox Jews today are equally controlled by many such rules which are not part of Scripture. Down the centuries different generations of teachers have given their interpretations of Scripture and then presented them as if they are Scripture itself.

After being criticized by the Pharisees for picking some ears of corn on the Sabbath, Jesus explained to them that the Sabbath was made for man, not man for the Sabbath. The pharisaical rules and regulations destroyed the reason why God had given the Sabbath in the first place. God intended it to be a time of re-creation – as well as a day of rest and worship.

Re-Creation

God intended recreation to be a time when we experience *re-creation*. We all need to do some things that are different from the normal activities of the working week. The old saying "All work and no play makes Jack a dull boy" expresses this very well. We all need involvement in other things in order to be lively, interesting people. For some people that will be involvement in watching or playing sport, for others it can be doing their garden, home decoration, reading, walking, fishing, playing a musical instrument, enjoying the family, walking the dog or any of a thousand and more hobbies and recreational activities.

In my work I have to spend a lot of time relating to people, so, for me, fishing is an ideal recreation, giving me space to find myself again after a period of intense activity. I am also fascinated by old cars, so much so that many years ago I wrote a *Complete Catalogue of British Cars*. Of course, my leadership role within Ellel Ministries is my primary calling before God, but I believe I am better equipped to do this work if I am able to enjoy some recreational activity as well.

We all need a means and a place where we can exercise our creative gifts, doing what we enjoy. God is the Creator, and if we spend time being creative, then we are being built up in the way God intended. Some people say to us that they are not creative. Sadly, that may be because they've believed what someone has said to them in the past, and they've grown up not thinking that they are able to do anything creative. On our special course called *Healing Through Creativity*, people can re-discover themselves and experience an enormous amount of healing and restoration as they begin to express the creativity that lies in the heart of every human being.

What Happens Through Recreation

The process of re-creation involves six different activities. If we can consciously use our recreation time to do these things, it will have a huge impact on our lives, making us more fully human and godlier in every way and better equipped to fulfill our destiny as children of God.

Re-covering

Psalm 91 tells us that *"He who dwells in the shelter [covering] of the Most High will rest in the shadow of the Almighty."* What an incredible promise this is! When we are tired, we need rest. When we've been stressed out, we need peace – we need to be continually dwelling in the shelter of God. When we've been tempted into sin we certainly haven't been under the covering of the Most High. I'm not thinking first of the more obvious sins, such as lust or greed, significant though these can be. I'm thinking more of the way that all human beings try to fix things in their own way. Instead of trusting God to show them His way, we take things into our own hands and move out from under the covering of the Most High.

Frank Sinatra used to sing that iconic twentieth-century song *"I did it my way"!* And when we do just that, thinking that we know better than God, then we are moving out from under the covering of God and if we carry on in that direction we will finish up under the covering of the enemy. And that's a dangerous place to be. So, one of the most important aspects of the Sabbath, or the Sunday, is to look hard at the events of the week that has passed and ask God to show you if and when you have done a *Sinatra* and lost the peace of God that's a fruit of His covering. Then it's only a simple step of repentance and of receiving forgiveness to get back into that covered place and be *re-covered*.

There may also be times during the week when you've done more than slipped out of cover, and through some specific sin you've blown a hole in the covering. The problem with an umbrella with holes is that you continue to get wet in the area where the holes are – and so does anyone else who is sharing your umbrella.

In a simple way this illustrates how important it is for parents not to blow holes in the cover for their children by sinning. For if they do, then the family could also be affected.

It says in Exodus 20:5, that the sins of the fathers will be visited on the children. We can only just touch on this important subject here, but if you sense this is a personal problem for you, then I would encourage you to read David Cross's book, *God's Covering* and as quickly as you can see where things went wrong, get *re-covered!*

Re-connecting

When we get absorbed in all the activities of the normal working week we can become detached from God. The pressures we are under and the need to meet the obligations to our employers and the expectations of others – at work, at home and even in church – can make us more and more dependent on our own ability to deliver the goods. The result can be physical exhaustion, but it can also spell danger spiritually. Then, there is the possibility of depression and various psychological and even psychiatric symptoms.

It's vital, therefore, that our times of recreation always incorporate times of spiritual refreshment with both God Himself and the family of God. Unless we feed our spirit we will remain spiritually drained and that will have a negative effect on every area of our life.

During my teenage years – those years when school seemed to be punctuated with an endless series of examinations – I was encouraged to follow the example of my father, who never used his Sunday as a day for work, whatever the pressures might have been. So I never touched my studies on the *Lord's Day*. The truth was, I was really glad of a day off, even though I was often tempted to "do a bit"! Even in the middle of examinations I never used Sunday as a day for study or even revision. Amazingly, my schoolwork never suffered. It was as if the complete break from studies was what my mental and bodily systems needed, in order to be much more efficient during the rest of the week.

I can see now how important those Sundays were to me. I was re-connecting with God and without even realizing it I was learning so much about Him through the teaching at church and Bible class. I would never have been able to do the work that has become my life's calling if, in my youth, Sunday had not been a day of re-connecting with God. I see them now as having been the most important days of my life.

Re-lating

When God created humanity He placed us in families. Relationships within our nuclear families are vital to our growth and development. During the early days of our lives most of what we learn, we learn from our parents. In several places in this book I have had reason to give thanks to my own mum and dad for all they put into my life through the relationships we had in the home. If parents don't consider their children important enough to spend time with them in the home, the children will look for input to their lives elsewhere.

Parents who don't spend time with their children are lighting the fuse of a time-bomb that one day could blow up in their faces. When parents share in their children's interests and children are encouraged to do things with their mum and dad, far more is happening than just the passage of time. Young lives are being taught, through relationships, some of the most important lessons of life.

Relationships with grandparents are also very important. Grandparents often have more time (if they are retired) to spend with their grandchildren. What a privilege it is when they are able to develop close and precious relationships with them.

Finally, and this may seem strange to some of you, but part of recreation is relating again to yourself! In several places the Psalmist says something like, *"Bless the Lord, O my soul..."* His spirit is relating afresh to his soul and telling it to get involved in worship. We all need personal time and space with ourselves, just being, reading, thinking, praying or whatever. I've noticed that in the lives of those people who don't know how to give themselves time and enjoy their own company it seems as though there's something missing, something not quite whole.

One of the signs of real maturity in a person's life is when they can be content to be with others and be equally content to be alone with themselves. When people can only be comfortable when they are at either end of the scale – either always with people or always by themselves – then it's obvious that something is out of balance and in need of healing.

Re-energizing

Without energy we can do nothing. Time off from work to rest, read, eat, fellowship, worship and enjoy all sorts of other activities, will re-energize us for life. Energy is not just supplied by the physical food that we eat – but spiritual food also plays its part. We are constantly drawing inspirational energy from our spirit, so if our spirit is refreshed, then our whole being will operate more effectively.

Re-envisioning

To fully appreciate a large painting you have to stand a significant distance away from the picture. If you're right up against the picture all you can see is the immediate detail, but you'll never catch the artist's vision for the whole painting.

It can be a bit like that with life. All the activities and routines which constitute life are a bit like the close-up detail of a great picture. We are deeply and intimately concerned about the little bit that's our personal responsibility and if we never have a break from it we will neither be able to catch a glimpse of the big picture nor be able to have fresh vision for the life God has called us to live. Sometimes we need a blank canvas on which to paint something new.

There are many occasions when I have walked away from the pressures for a time of *re-creation* and then discovered that suddenly God gives me fresh vision for something important. If I hadn't pulled away from the detail I would never have been able to see the big picture that God wanted me to pray about and then walk into. The temptation is to think that time away from your responsibilities is time wasted – in reality it's the very opposite. Unless you have time away from them, you'll never be free to be re-envisioned. God often surprises me by suddenly showing me something really important while I'm walking the dog, watching a football match or fishing.

Re-equipping

When a ship has been at sea for a considerable period of time, its owners eventually take it out of service for a time so that it can be re-fitted and re-equipped for a further period of sea-going adventures. But while it's at sea the crew are always giving constant attention to all the routine maintenance.

A few years ago my wife and I were blessed to be able to go on a short cruise to the West Indies. While we were enjoying a time ashore in Barbados, some of the crew were suspended over the side of the vessel in a cradle, painting the sides of the ship. Every available opportunity was used to ensure that the vessel was kept in the best possible condition.

The regular weekly times of recreation are a little like the regular maintenance of the vessel that's continually carried out throughout the life of the ship. But there may come a time when it's necessary to take a longer period out, for a time of personal re-evaluation of life and then re-equipping for the next period of service.

In Ellel Ministries we do a number of longer courses called Schools. The Flagship School covers nine weeks. The whole curriculum is designed to help people look afresh at every area of their faith and life. Many then go on to do a second, third and even fourth stage on our NETS training program at Ellel Pierrepont. On every school we find that as many as 30 or 40 per cent of the people are using this training opportunity a little like the owners of a great ship use such a time for re-equipping the vessel when in the dock.

Increasingly we are discovering that people have set out on a career, only to discover that their chosen career came to an abrupt end somewhere in the middle of life. For some it's a great shock, for others it can be a relief. But all are asking the question, "What do I do next?" Taking a longer time out with God in the middle of life can be a totally life-transforming experience. It can also test our faith as we suddenly realize we have to trust God for His direction in our lives and sometimes trust Him to take us into an entirely new arena of living.

We are constantly amazed at what God begins to do with people in the next phase of their life after they've given God the space and the time to hear His voice and be equipped for the future. Some of their testimonies have been quite astounding. So don't feel that if life seems to have fallen apart halfway through that this is the end of the road as far as your life in God is concerned. It is more likely to be the very opposite – the beginning of a whole new adventure with Him as you are re-equipped once again as a sea-going vessel!

Summary

Unless we build rest and re-creation time into the regular schedules of our lives there will come a time when we'll be so stressed out that we won't be able to continue. Something will give way and then we will have a much more difficult job on our hands to get back into the place of safety and security that God wants us to enjoy in Him.

CHAPTER 16

THE FINAL JOURNEY

I was just about to write this chapter when we got a telephone message. The oldest member of our ministry team at Ellel Grange had just been taken to hospital following a suspected brain hemorrhage. I immediately went down to the hospital where Bobby now was. I met with his wife, Grace, and their daughters in a visitors' room and we prayed together as we waited for news. At ninety-one years of age it was clear that this was the beginning of Bobby's final home-call.

Following a scan, the doctors confirmed the diagnosis. They said there was nothing that could be done and that they had made him comfortable. When we gathered round Bobby at his bedside, he was breathing deeply, but not obviously aware of our presence. He was at peace.

When a person is in a coma, they may not be conscious but it is important to remember that the spirit never goes unconscious. Consciousness is a function of the soul and the body, so you can always speak to the spirit of an unconscious person. As we gathered round Bobby we thanked God for his long life, for his strong faith and his clear testimony to the Lord Jesus. We

spoke words of encouragement into his spirit as Bobby was preparing to "cross the river," from being alive in God's Kingdom
in this world to being alive for eternity in the glorious presence
of the Lord Jesus.

Bobby never regained consciousness in this world. About
7.30 p.m., with Grace at his side, we gently released Bobby into
the presence of the Lord. At 8.00 p.m. *"the silver cord"* was broken (Ecclesiastes 12:6–7), and Bobby's spirit returned to God as
he breathed his last breath here on earth. At times like this we
realize that to know the Savior personally is more important than
anything else on earth.

This is the moment when we say that someone has died.
But the very word "death" speaks of an ending when, in reality,
it is the moment of release into an incredible new beginning.
Conception is the gateway through which we enter time. Death
is the gateway through which we enter into the timelessness
of eternity. For those of us who are in Christ, the moment that
we call death is the most exciting moment of our existence, as
we traverse the horizon of what we can see, into the land that
can only be seen from here by faith.

As my own brother lay dying a few years ago, he said it was
like waiting on the platform of a station for a train to come in – a
train which was stopping to pick up only one passenger! It was
a train that was coming because God had sent it and it was a train
that had an eternal destination.

The Peace of God

It was so obvious that as Bobby died, he was experiencing the
peace of God, which really does pass all understanding, during
his time of transition from earth to heaven. This isn't always the
case, however. I have known people at that time of impending
death to be in a torment of uncertainty.

One of the early advisors to the work of Ellel Ministries was the matron of a terminal care hospice. She often talked to me about the experiences people went through as their time of parting approached. For many, it was far from a time of peace – it was a time of torment, as fear for the future became their dominant experience. In others it was obvious that there was strong demonic power operating in their bodies – powers which opposed all attempts at bringing the peace of Jesus into their lives and from which people needed deliverance.

On our Healing Retreats we help people face the realities of their lives. We help them to deal with the consequences of unforgiven sin, relationships that need to be healed and the pain caused by rejection or abuse. We help them to repent of their involvement in ungodly things such as the occult, drugs or pornography. The enemy tries to use all of these things to keep us away from that place of peace.

I well remember one man who came on such a Healing Retreat. When he arrived he was already in the advanced stages of terminal cancer. His counselors were not lacking in faith for healing. But they sensed God was asking them to prepare this man for dying. This was his time. His wife was with him throughout the experience.

The ministry team prayed through all the issues of his life. There were many things lying beneath the surface which had caused him much inner distress. Little by little God brought him healing and deliverance and he left the retreat still with the cancer, but a very different man indeed.

He passed away ten days later and shortly after that I had a letter from his widow. She said, "Don't let anyone say that my husband wasn't healed on the retreat. The last ten days of his life were the best ten days of our marriage – he died a healed man!" He had experienced the life-transforming peace of God.

Death – Part of Life!

As the writer of Ecclesiastes says (chapter 3:2), there is "a time to be born and a time to die." But just as we cannot decide when to be conceived, the exact moment of our death is something that we can never anticipate. We can't know when our last day on earth will come. That's why we should always be ready. It's a strange paradox that we need to live our lives to the full here on earth, but always be ready to step on the train when it comes for us.

My first encounter with death came as a child. A little girl who lived just down the road from us had been killed in a terrible accident. My parents tried to shield me from what had happened, but I remember staring at the stained spot on the road where she had been run over and wondering where my little friend had gone.

A little later, aged nine, I stood with my older brother by my grandfather's bedside. I didn't know that Grandpa was so sick and dying of a kidney disease. I can see him now, painfully taking two two-shilling pieces from his purse and giving one each to my brother and I – his last gift to his only grandchildren – and then praying for us both. I found it a little strange, for before then he had never given us more than a sixpence (and that was a lot of money for him) and it was the first time he had prayed for us in this way. He died the following day. I could never bring myself to spend the money and I still have my two-shilling piece! A two-shilling piece is only 10p in today's English money, but it was worth a great deal more in 1953. These times were all part of growing up as I realized that life and death are both part of human experience.

For those who suffer long-term physical conditions which are known to be life-threatening, death is an ever-present possibility, which helps to focus attention on realities. In these circumstances people have time to prepare themselves for that most important day of their lives. Sadly, most people in these circumstances will try and move heaven and earth to remain on earth a bit longer. But few seem interested in wanting to know the God of Heaven whilst they are still here on earth.

There are many people, however, who don't have the privilege of a time of preparation. They suddenly find themselves facing death in circumstances that are beyond their control. Heart attacks, accidents, acts of terrorism or war, and dozens of other possibilities, can face us unexpectedly on any day of our lives. I was in Toronto airport on the 11th September 2001. Suddenly the check-in desks were closed down as all flights out of North America were cancelled. None of the 3,000 people who died when the World Trade Towers collapsed expected that to be their last day on earth.

Life is wonderful, but it can also be very uncertain. It's vital, therefore, that even if death should take us by surprise, we are always in a state of readiness, knowing the certainty of our eventual destination when the train finally stops at our station. For that moment of death is never a surprise for God.

Being Ready When Death Comes

The most certain thing we can say about anyone's life is that one day he or she will die (1 Corinthians 15:21–22). This is the ultimate reality of life from the moment of birth, and even from the time of conception. Death entered into the human race at the fall of man and every single human being who has existed on this planet has had to live with the curse of death being their ultimate earthly experience. Sin separated us from God and it was because of that separation that God sent His Son to die in our place. He who had no sin was not subject to death, so, for Jesus, the resurrection to eternal life was certain. (*See the first four chapters of this book.*)

The only way we can prepare for the experience of dying is to enter now into the experience of living in Jesus. For He is our only eternal guarantee. As I meditated on the passing of my dear friend Bobby, I realized once again how utterly critical it is that we should consider the claims of Jesus now, while we are alive and still have time to get to know the Savior. He's the only one who can take us safely through the curtain of death, giving us confidence and hope.

My wife's father had just enjoyed his Sunday lunch. He sat down with his Bible and began to read from the book of Revelation, telling his wife how wonderful were the preparations God had made for those who know the Lord. She got up to make a cup of coffee and returned a few minutes later to find his body still sitting there, holding the open Bible. But he had gone! His final home call came just as he was thinking about what God had prepared for him. He was ready to meet his Maker.

My own dad died suddenly also. I'd enjoyed a lovely evening with both mum and dad and set off home from the hotel they were staying at. My last words to dad and his last words to me were *"Goodbye"* as I gave him a kiss through the open window of the car. I drove off, but seconds later he was in the immediate presence of his Lord. I had no mobile phone in those days so it was a good hour before I heard the news.

Dad had dropped to the floor near where my car had been parked, leaving my mother on her knees next to him as he was dying. What a trauma for my mother – except that God had even planned special support for her at that moment of his final home-call.

Many years earlier Dad had offered some fishing to the son of a man he had met in Scotland. Dad never forgot how important it was to build relationships with people as a means of sharing the gospel. The boy's father, also called Peter, never forgot that encounter and was always grateful.

On the night Dad died, Peter just happened to be visiting the house next to the very place where my father died. As he left the house, at the precise time of my mum's great need, he almost stumbled over this lady, kneeling by a man on the floor. He was astounded that he knew them both and my mum was astounded that, in her moment of desperation, the very first person that should come to her aid was a friend from years ago whom she last met 400 miles away from where she now was!

Providence can be defined as God's advance preparation for today's need. God had carefully prepared for my dad's parting from this world. I had the perfect opportunity to say goodbye – my last words to him – and mum was not left without support. My dad often used to say, *"God's clocks keep perfect time."* Even in his death God provided a perfect illustration of His timely provision.

Death doesn't always come with such suddenness and physical peace, for there are many people, believers too, who die in difficult circumstances at the end of long illnesses. The wife of one of our Trustees was in the latter stages of cancer. While we prayed everything we knew, the cancer continued to grow in her body till there came a time when it was obvious that her body was declining at a faster rate than the medical treatment could handle. Yet, in the midst of this she never ceased to love and praise God and to worship Him.

Through this time the Lord taught us a very important lesson. Even in death there can be abundant life! She went to be with her Lord in the abundance of resurrection life – with a failing body but with an undimmed spirit, rejoicing in the certain knowledge of her destination.

On another occasion I received a telephone call in the very early hours of the morning. It was a pastor friend telling me the awful news that their daughter, in her mid-twenties, had just stopped breathing and had died. I was dressed in seconds and was

at their house in less than ten minutes. During the short car journey to their home I was praying with great urgency for God to
give me the right words to say and show me what He wanted me
to do. I wondered even if I should be praying for a resurrection?

I jumped out of the car, knocked on the door of their house,
which was opened seconds later, and suddenly out of my lips
came the words of Scripture, totally unprepared and unrehearsed,
*"The Lord gave and the Lord has taken away; Blessed be the name of
the Lord"* (Job 1:21, NASB). I didn't need to think about what to
say or do, the Holy Spirit had filled my mouth with God's words
for that moment. We know that all our times are in His hands
(Psalm 31:15). In this case God had taken their precious daughter
to be with Himself. We were able to gather round her body and
commit her to the Lord in absolute trust and confidence. At the
same time her parents received comfort from the Lord beyond
that which any human being could bring.

We knew the intimacy of the Lord's presence in those precious moments, which I will never forget as long as I live. As we
looked down at her body, all that could come from our lips was
thanksgiving to God for her life. She loved her Lord dearly, had
spent her short years in serving Him and telling others about
Him – now she was enjoying the richness of His presence. Those
were holy moments of both tears and thanksgiving.

Life – a Preparation for Death

God has an eternal Kingdom, and His desire is to enjoy fellowship with the redeemed for ever in heaven. All of life is a time of
preparation for what is to come. How we spend life "here" will
determine how and where we spend life "there."

It's all too easy in the midst of life's pressures and pain to lose
sight of this vital eternal dimension. As the writer of the Hebrews
said, *"here we do not have an enduring city, but we are looking for the*

city that is to come" (Hebrews 13:14). Everything of this world will be left behind. We can take nothing physical with us. When the spirit finally leaves the body all that was ours – wealth, home, possessions – is left behind. It is how we live our short span of life here on earth that determines so much about our life in eternity.

Although most people don't realize it, we've been building in this life for an eternity beyond. It's how we have lived here that determines our eternal destiny. Paul tells us this so clearly in 1 Corinthians 3:10–15. Will what we have been building survive the fire of God's judgment? Paul says that some people will enter eternity thankful for the salvation won for them by Jesus – but that everything else will be consumed. Paul teaches here that there is a direct correlation between the way we live here on earth and the eternal treasure that is laid up for us in heaven.

The story of the wealthy man who managed to get into heaven, but who was only shown by St Peter to the most humble of accommodation, is certainly in accord with the teaching of Scripture. When the man complained about the size of his accommodation, St Peter is said to have replied that it was the best they could do with what had been sent on in advance! It's only a story, but a similar sentiment is expressed by Jesus in the parable of the talents, where those who had wisely used (invested) the things that God had given them, were rewarded greatly (Matthew 25:14–30).

Preparing to Die

It's amazing how shy people are of considering the fact of their own future death. But let's be real about this taboo subject. One day it will be on the agenda for your life and mine. God's plans for our life not only embrace our years in time but the joy of eternity also.

To be at peace with both God and man we should never live with the burden of unfinished business. My Great-Uncle Will died the day after his birthday. He had served the Lord all his days and had always followed this maxim to the limit of his ability. He had received various birthday presents from the family and before he went to bed that night he faithfully penned his thank-you letters to all who had sent him cards and gifts. We received his thank-you letter for the present my mum and dad had given him at the same time as the telephone call to say that he had died! He was right up to date with everything, even his thank-you letters, when his home-call came.

But thank-you letters are trivial matters when compared with the big issues of life that people often fail to resolve while they still have time. It would be wise from time to time to consider life in a wider context than today's pressures and responsibilities. Ask the Lord to show you if there is anything you need to do now, that you would regret not having done if your life should suddenly come to an end.

Of course, this exercise is important in terms of our relationships with other human beings, but it's also of eternal importance in terms of our relationship with God. Those who are involved in pastoral work are often surprised by the unconfessed sins which can come tumbling out of the heart of the dying. Every time this happens I wonder why they have hung on to these things for so long, with all their consequences – making life miserable for themselves and, often, denying others the joy of resolution of sometimes life-long relationship issues. We should seek to live at all times as if we're going to have a long life and yet be ready for eternity should this be our last day on earth!

Summary

Death is the only certainty in life. Christians have nothing to fear from death. As Paul said, "Where, O death, is your victory? Where, O death, is your sting?" (1 Corinthians 15:55). We need to live as if every day is our last so that when we do die there will be no unfinished business between God and ourselves.

CHAPTER 17

PROSPECTS OF GLORY

In the last chapter we faced the reality of dying – but now I want to look at the joy of eternal living!

In days gone by, when a young man left school and entered a career, his parents would want to know if the position had prospects. The significance of the question is that if he would have to "start at the bottom," would there, in time, be the opportunity for promotion to a more senior and more well-rewarded position within the firm? The seniority of the person offering the position and the apparent success of the business were seen as evidence that there were opportunities to be looked forward to. What could be seen gave them a sense of security for the unseen future.

We all like to have evidence before committing ourselves, whether we are committing ourselves to an investment, the booking of a holiday or the start of a career. We weigh the evidence and, if convinced, we then take the risk. As far as a holiday is concerned we're always glad to have a report from someone who has been to the place we're thinking of going to. Their first-hand account is worth much more than advertising copy from a company who is trying to sell you the holiday.

And as far as heaven and our prospects for eternity are concerned, a first-hand account from someone who has been there is worth much more than a million guesses at what heaven might be like, from those who have pioneered the many different religions. One of the strongest pieces of evidence against the supposed truth of any of the non-biblical religions is that they all tell you very different things about the after-life. The Hindu, Buddhist and Moslem ideas of life after death and of how to enter heaven are all so different from each other that one can only conclude that these accounts are not first-hand reports of someone who has been there. They can only be fabrications.

And yet, in spite of the confusing message that the different religions give, I believe that most people, whether or not they are believers in Jesus, instinctively know that there is more to life than what can be seen and experienced here on earth. Surveys of popular beliefs consistently reveal that as many as 70 per cent of the population believe there is a God and that there is life after death. A large recent survey published in the *Boston Globe* stated that 98 per cent of people believed in life after death and 74 per cent believe in heaven. The wonder of the Christian message is that we have a Savior who came from heaven's glory, so we don't have to speculate about heaven's existence or wonder what it's going to be like. We have an eye-witness.

There's only one human being who, to date, has ever experienced life in heaven. His name is Jesus and He has given us first-hand testimony to its existence and given us some very important information about what it's going to be like. The difference between Christianity and every other religion is that believers in Jesus are trusting in the One who has come from heaven, whilst believers in every other religion are trusting in a belief which has begun in the heart of man.

Christianity is the story of God's search for relationship with man whereas every other religion is the search of man after God.

Man was deceived at the Fall and, ever since, Satan has ensured that man continues to be deceived about the most important issues of life – and, of course, death. Yes, God has put eternity in the heart of every human being, so that He will want to search after God, but man's search for God can only be fulfilled when it is met by God's search for man. Jesus Christ, the Son of God, stands at that point of meeting and His coming into the world has divided history for two thousand years.

Leonardo da Vinci's famous painting of the creation of Adam shows the finger of God stretching down to earth, and just touching the end of Adam's finger, which is stretching up to heaven. It perfectly matches the imagery and revelation of Scripture. Jesus came from heaven's glory to reveal to us what the Father is like, be the sacrifice for our sins and demonstrate living evidence that those who believe in Him *have prospects* in eternity.

He's Preparing a Place

Not only did Jesus tell us about heaven, but He also drew us a map to show us how to get there. Most car drivers now have a satellite navigation system built into their vehicle. All you have to do is key in your destination and the *SatNav (GPS)* will calculate exactly where you are now and in seconds it will prepare a route to get you from here to there. Not only that, but a voice (in tones of your own choosing!), will tell you at every junction just which way to go in order to reach your chosen destination.

When Jesus went back to heaven He sent His Holy Spirit to the Church and for the past two thousand years the Holy Spirit has been the voice from on high to lead us day by day through our earthly life, until we safely arrive at our heavenly destination. A song we sang as children at Sunday School asked the question, *"Do you want a pilot?"* Assuming that the answer was to be "yes," the second line urged us to *"Signal then to Jesus and bid Him come on board."*

The end of the song gave the assurance that with Jesus on board the ship of our lives, *"He will safely guide, until we reach, at last, the heavenly harbor."* Simple words, yes, but deliberately written so that children can understand the message. The message, however, is incredibly profound. If only adult men and women, who so often prefer to do it in their own way, would lay down their pride and accept the simple truth that it's only when we go His way that we will always finish up at the right destination.

It was this simple, yet profound, understanding that Jesus was seeking to impart to His disciples in John 14. At the beginning of His ministry, when the crowds were clamoring for His teaching, healing and deliverance ministry, things were going so well. The disciples' attention was totally absorbed by each day's activities. But the situation for Jesus was changing. The tide had turned against Him. The Pharisees hated Him and were now making threats against His life. How were the disciples going to cope with having followed Him faithfully for three years, if they then discovered that all they had hoped for proved fruitless?

The disciples must have asked Jesus hundreds of questions in their three years of walking with Him. But now that the pressure was on, Jesus was already trying to comfort and encourage them by answering the questions, perhaps unspoken, about the future. Jesus knew that He was going to die – and even the disciples must have suspected that something like this might happen. The prospects at that time looked pretty grim. Jesus had already predicted His betrayal and even that Simon Peter would deny Him. Now the disciples were in disarray.

It was into this very tense situation that you can hear the quiet but strong voice of Jesus speaking to His beloved disciples, *"Do not let your hearts be troubled. Trust in God, trust also in me. In my*

Father's house are many rooms; if it were not so, I would have told you. I am going there to prepare a place for you." You can almost sense the hush descending on the group, as they tried to take in what Jesus was saying. He had come from heaven's glory and now He who knew what heaven was like, was describing it as a place with rooms for all God's people.

Then Jesus came out with that most comforting of truths – "I'm coming back!" His actual words were, *"And if I go and prepare a place for you, I will come back and take you to be with me that you also may be where I am."* Not only was Jesus going back to heaven, one day He was going to come back for all who would be counted as children of God. John said in chapter 1 and verse 12 of his Gospel, that *"to all who received him...he gave the right to become children of God!"* What a promise, and what a privilege – eternity in heaven, with God, thanks to Jesus.

But then it was Thomas who spoke up on behalf of all of us when he said, *"Lord, we don't know where you are going, so how can we know the way?"* It was in answer to this very practical question that Jesus gave the most condensed and simple summary of the whole Christian gospel. *"I am the way,"* He said, *"and the truth and the life. No-one comes to the Father except through me."*

Yes, Jesus is coming back again, but how can we live so that we don't get lost on the journey? And how can those who will die before Jesus returns be sure that they're on the right road? One of the most famous of all Christian books, *The Pilgrim's Progress,* written in the seventeenth century by John Bunyan, paints a remarkable picture of Christian's journey from the City of Destruction to the gates of the Celestial City, describing the many pitfalls there are along the way.

Bunyan wonderfully illustrates from Scripture how, if we follow Jesus, and obey what He has already said, we will be able to stay on the path to glory. The path may be narrow, and often fraught with attacks from the powers of darkness, but it will eventually take us to that place, where, at last, we'll wait for God's call to cross the river and enter the gates of the heavenly city.

Bunyan's imagery is remarkable, and his faithfulness to Scripture is total. *The Pilgrim's Progress* is still an important book for Christians to read and I, personally, have reason to give thanks to God for the many times when stories from the book have helped me on my own journey or given me illustrations to use in my preaching and teaching ministry.

There are countless thousands, probably millions, of people the world over for whom Bunyan has set an extraordinary example of how to interpret the words of Jesus to His disciples and remain faithful to following Him along the Way. One of the first descriptions of believers, used by Saul (before he became Paul) to describe the people he was seeking to imprison and kill, was *"those who belonged to the Way"* or *"the people of the Way"* (Acts 9:1–2).

The focus of all the characters on Bunyan's journey, who are truly of the Way, is heaven's glory – the gates of the Celestial City. It's that focus on the reality of what Jesus and the Word of God have already revealed that constantly draws them on and gives them the strength to continue persevering through life's journey, whatever the ups and downs of life for them may be. And having crossed the final river (of death) they are greeted by angels – the *"ministering spirits sent to serve those who will inherit salvation"* (Hebrews 1:14).

These angels tell Christian, and his friend Hopeful, of the wonders of the heavenly Jerusalem. Already they are experiencing some of the blessings, for they left behind their mortal clothing in the river and are now re-clothed in the unstained garments of heaven. The cloak of sin has finally gone, the powers of darkness have been defeated and the last hold of the enemy on them has been released.

Divine Revelation

The last book of the Bible is all prophecy. Throughout its pages there is a progressive revelation of the future as John describes all that the angel sent by Jesus showed him. The book begins with the words, *"The revelation of Jesus Christ."* These are not words dreamed up by any human agency, but given by Jesus Himself to John to conclude the Scriptures and provide eternal encouragement to the saints as they press on in their pilgrimage.

Throughout the book of Revelation there are descriptions of different aspects of heaven and also of the events that must happen before the final winding up of the ages takes place at the end of time. Revelation is not only a book of joy for believers, it's also a rock of offence for those who choose not to believe. For the book of Revelation also tells of the final judgment of those who have not chosen to follow Jesus. John explains how only those whose names are written in the Lamb's book of life will be entitled to enter heaven (Revelation 21:27). For, then *"the dwelling of God is with men, and he will live with them. They will be his people and God himself will be with them and be their God"* (Revelation 21:3).

The promises of God about heaven are rich and full of comfort for the believer. Jesus said, *"It is done. I am the Alpha and the Omega, the beginning of the End. To him who is thirsty I will give to drink, without cost from the spring of the water of life. He who overcomes will inherit all this, and I will be his God and he will be my son"* (Revelation 21:6–7).

Then John describes the extraordinary beauty and richness of the new Jerusalem. He describes the gates of pearl and the streets of transparent gold. He explains that the city didn't need the sun or moon for lighting, for the *"glory of God gives it light"* (Revelation 21:23). And flowing from the throne of God and of the Lamb is the river of the water of life – wonderful imagery describing extraordinary truth.

I have only given here a few scattered references from the book to what heaven is going to be like – there's so much more. I urge you to read it for yourself, allowing your spirit to enter into the revelation that was given to John so that you and I would know the truth. God ensured that the words of Revelation would stand for all of time as His final witness to all that would come to pass:

"I, Jesus, have sent my angel to give you this testimony for the churches. I am the Root and the Offspring of David, and the bright Morning Star. The Spirit and the bride say, 'Come!' And let him who hears say, 'Come!' Whoever is thirsty, let him come; and whoever wishes, let him take the free gift of the water of life." (Revelation 22:16–17)

And then, right at the end of the book Jesus says, *"Yes, I am coming soon."* To which all believers can respond with joy, *"Amen. Come, Lord Jesus"* (Revelation 22:20).

Prospects Indeed!

It's abundantly clear from Scripture that all true believers in the Lord Jesus have wonderful prospects. Prospects that will exceed anything that even the richest and most powerful of human beings has ever enjoyed on earth – prospects that aren't dependent on our wealth or our achievements, but on the finished work of Jesus upon the cross.

John the Baptist described Jesus as the Lamb of God who would take away the sin of the world. In Revelation we see the Lamb upon the throne in heaven and the redeemed of the Lord rejoicing in their salvation, as they sing in worship of their Savior and their Redeemer:

"Worthy is the Lamb, who was slain, to receive power and wealth and wisdom and strength and honour and glory and praise!"

and

'To Him who sits on the throne and to the Lamb, be praise and honour and glory and power, for ever and ever.' (Revelation 5:12, 13)

Whilst heaven will rightfully be filled with praise and worship to Almighty God, I have no doubt also that heaven is going to be a very exciting place. A place where we will see all that God intended for man, before the Fall, being fulfilled in ways that are beyond our imagination. It will be a place where we are more fulfilled than we could ever be on earth, a place of joy and a place of destiny. I'm looking forward to being there and sharing in the joy of the redeemed with all those who know and love the Lord Jesus!

Summary

Jesus came from heaven and showed us what the Father is like. He is a God who fulfills His promises and can be trusted. We can trust, therefore, all the promises of God about life beyond the grave. What a prospect all of us who know the Lord can look forward to. It is the inheritance we can claim because of Jesus.

CHAPTER 18

PRESSING ON!

Whenever the Olympic Games are on, I am glued to the television screen. I love it, every minute of it. I don't get bored with watching all the re-runs of great achievements. And being British, whenever the British team excel, I can't help but get excited. At times I am unable to speak because of the emotion of the occasion!

In the 2008 Olympics, when Nicole Cook got the first British gold medal in the long-distance cycling event or Rebecca Adlington got two amazing gold medals in the swimming pool, a hopeless case of national pride and emotion combined to render me speechless! On returning to the UK, the whole British team were treated as national heroes.

The supreme star of the athletics events in recent Olympic Games has been that long-legged Jamaican, Usain Bolt. I totally empathized with the people we saw on the streets of Jamaica, as the whole island erupted and went into celebration at their star athlete's three gold medals. Usain Bolt was king of the running track in the high-profile sprint events.

I watched these and many other scenes from around the world as people from various different countries celebrated their team's achievements. As the awards were handed out and the national anthems were played, one athlete after another couldn't hold in their emotions as they stood on the podium, with their medals around their necks and tears flowing down their cheeks!

The Race of Life

Suddenly, even as I was watching, I realized my attention had drifted away and my thoughts were focusing on a very different event – not an athletic performance for which people were receiving an earthly reward – but the end of the race of life, when each of us comes to the finishing line of our personal race. There was one race that reminded me of the heavenly award ceremony.

Nicole Cook's gold medal in the Beijing Olympics was an extraordinary achievement. She had been in the leading pack throughout her grueling race. She had given her best, but with the finishing line in sight she had disappeared from the leading group and four riders were sprinting to the line to claim the medals. Nicole was not among them. Then suddenly, seemingly out of nowhere, another rider came round the final bend and was bearing down on the leading pack.

Nicole had carefully prepared herself for the event. The final yards of the race were all uphill and uphill cycling was her great strength. She knew that all her other challengers would be trying to give their all as they pushed to the line, but would have to slow down as the hill sapped the energy from their legs. Her moment had come. She kept her best for the last.

With every muscle straining to its absolute limit she pressed home her advantage, but she was so far behind the leading four that victory seemed impossible. But Nicole knew exactly what she was doing and what she was capable of. She had carefully surveyed the track and the uphill climb to the finishing line. As the others tired, she streaked past them and at the finishing line the wheel of her bike was just ahead of all the others. She had pressed on to the end – and the gold medal was hers! She had finished well.

The Apostle Paul was determined to finish well in his personal race of life. He had pushed himself to the limit for the sake of the gospel. He had traversed the known world to preach and teach about Jesus. Wherever he had gone, people had become Christians, churches had been founded and the Kingdom of God had been built on earth. It would have been easy, even justified, for him to have sat back, saying, "I've done my bit – now it's over to you" as he wrote or spoke to the younger leaders of the developing Church.

But these were precious days, perhaps even Paul's most important days. He still had life in his body and, therefore, some time to press home the advantage of all his experience to teach and train the Body of Christ. He had no intention of giving up before he crossed his own personal finishing line. Even when imprisoned, at the very end of his days, he used his pen to put precious teaching in writing so that all generations of Christians, including our own, could benefit from everything the Lord had taught him in his years as a missionary pioneer.

There were great achievements to his credit – many "gold medals" that had been won – yet when he wrote to the Philippians he still said, *"I press on to take hold of that for which Christ Jesus took hold of me"* (Philippians 3:12). Paul knew that there was a destiny calling on his life and there was still part of the journey, the race of life, to be run. God had called Paul to Himself for a purpose and the clock was still ticking!

Then he said, *"Brothers, I do not consider myself yet to have taken hold of it. But one thing I do: Forgetting what is behind and straining toward what is ahead, I press on towards the goal to win the prize for which God has called me heavenwards in Christ Jesus."*

For Paul, his finishing line was in sight. He was conscious of
the heavenward call that was soon to come from on high, but
he was still straining to fulfill his destiny here on earth while
there was still breath in his lungs. All the successes of the past
were yesterday's achievements. They had been very important
then, but now they no longer mattered. What mattered to Paul
was "what is God asking of me today?"

The Blessings of Obedience

"What is God asking of me today?" is, ultimately, the only question that matters every single day of our lives. In the Old Testament we learned that "To obey is better than sacrifice" (1 Samuel
15:22). Yes, the formalities of our faith are important, and in Samuel's day that involved sacrifices. But we need to be very clear on
this one, we can do all the religious things we like, but if we're
not doing that which God has asked us to do we're missing the
mark. The sacrifices were irrelevant if the life of the one making
the sacrifices was out of line with God.

In Philippians 2:5 Paul emphasized that we need to have the
same attitude as the one Jesus had. This should be a hallmark of
our Christian lives. For Jesus this meant *"taking on the nature of a
servant"* and serving those God had sent Him to save. And whilst
we, as the children of God, are the community of the redeemed,
that doesn't exempt us from also being servants of the living God
and, therefore, servants of all those to whom God sends us.

In this truth there is great joy. For, ultimately, not only has
God got our interests at heart, but He also knows how we can be
most fruitful for the Kingdom. So to be obedient to God is good
for us as well as being good for God. It's a win-win position to
be in!

Paul had learnt his own personal lessons well and now, by
his example, he was teaching the young leaders of his day. But he

wasn't only teaching those young leaders – he was teaching the Church for all of time, that the purposes of God for each one of our lives will not cease while we still have breath.

In Chapter 16 I told of the passing into glory of Bobby – he was the oldest member of our Ellel Grange ministry team at the time. But with declining health there came a time a few years earlier when he no longer had the strength to be involved in the counseling and healing ministry. So he retired from the ministry team. But did he retire from God's service? Not at all. He and his wife Grace committed themselves to pray every single day for the Ellel leaders and teams around the world, who teach and minister in so many different countries.

Fiona and I have often sensed being carried round the world on the cushion of their prayers. Bobby was faithful in his commitment to prayer for the team right up to the very last day of his life. He and Grace pressed on to fulfill that for which God had called them to Himself in the first place. Not one day of his life was unfruitful for the Kingdom. What a blessing. But now Bobby has run his race and is enjoying the anthems of heaven in praise of the Lamb of God. He's not wearing a medal round his neck, but a golden crown instead (2 Timothy 4:8).

Paul said in his final letter to Timothy (2 Timothy 4:7–8), *"the time has come for my departure. I have fought the good fight, I have finished the race, I have kept the faith. Now there is in store for me the crown of righteousness, which the Lord, the righteous judge, will award to me on that day – and not only to me, but also to all who have longed for his appearing."*

Such a crown will be ours one day, but for now our responsibility is to press on to complete the race and not give up before the end. In this race, we aren't competing against other people; we are running to achieve the purposes of God for our lives. Our personal race is simply to fulfill the destiny God has laid out for us.

Let Us Run with Perseverance

The author of a recent book expressed surprise at how many Christian leaders failed to finish well. They had served God for most of their lives but, it seems, as soon as they took their focus off their calling, they fell victim to a variety of problems. Some went into deception, some had wrong relationships, some even lost their faith.

Paul knew of these dangers – no wonder he talked on so many occasions about the need to press on and persevere, to demonstrate endurance and to keep going until the finishing line had been crossed. There's little point in getting enthusiastic about some exciting meetings if there isn't the solidity of faith and relationship with God to take you through to the end of the race.

Paul even warned about the need to endure hardship! The Christian life may be glorious, but we are not exempt from hard times. Indeed, one might even say that the more glorious our experience of God, the more likely we are to come under attack from the enemy of souls. Oh, how important it is that we don't relax, drop our guard and lose our focus on the reason why God called us to Himself.

Hebrews 11 is an amazing catalogue of the heroes and heroines of faith from the Old Testament. They are those who have gone before. Since then, they have been joined by countless other saints in glory – saints who are described by the author of Hebrews as a cloud of witnesses. They are watching those who are still running the race. I often sense the encouragement of the generations gone by to keep on running and not to give up.

For the writer of Hebrews, the faith of those who have gone before is a spur to throw off every hindrance, and every sinful entanglement, that gets in the way of our calling and destiny. He uses the picture of an athlete running a race and says, *"let us run with perseverance the race marked out for us"* (Hebrews 12:1.)

Then using the example of Jesus as our ultimate encouragement he says, *"Let us fix our eyes on Jesus, the author and perfecter of our faith, who for the joy set before him endured the cross, scorning its shame, and sat down at the right hand of the throne of God. **Consider him** who endured such opposition from sinful men, so that you will not grow weary and lose heart"* (Hebrews 12:2–3, emphasis added).

Consider Him . . .

Jesus received a unique commission from Father God. He was called from heaven's glory to be the Redeemer of sinful mankind – to be your Redeemer, and mine. At all times He had free will – free will either to carry on with His commission or to call on the legions of angels and be released from the reason why He came.

There must have been many occasions when to escape would have been very attractive – especially on that night before He was crucified. In the Garden of Gethsemane, He faced the reality of what obedience was going to cost. At that point He chose to ignore the twelve legions of angels and to drink of the "cup" that was being placed into His hand.

It was His ultimate test. Tomorrow did not promise to be an easy day. He knew what was at stake – the salvation of mankind – and there was a price to be paid. He chose to pay that price and to press through to victory.

It's easy to begin something – it's much harder to complete what you set out to do. All of us could begin a twenty-six-mile marathon race. But not many would finish it unless they'd had many months of training and preparation. It's easy to preach a challenging message and see hundreds of people deciding to serve the Lord. But I have often wondered how many of these sincere people will still be there in their place of service when the cost of following Jesus begins to be felt.

God's not looking for people who will start the race, but soon give up. He's looking for a strength of faith and integrity which says I will finish what God inspires me to begin – whatever the cost. For Jesus there was suffering, but it was followed by joy. Paul, like tens of thousands of people today, said, *"I want to know Christ and the power of his resurrection"* (Philippians 3:10). But unlike Paul, many of today's crowds who are impressed by power are not so willing to walk the road Jesus walked, in order to experience the joy. It was a road of suffering!

It's a strange fact that only by dying to ourselves can we ever know the fullness of Life. The road of blessing is a road of sacrifice. It's a road of laying down the ungodly, selfish motives of the heart and choosing only to be motivated by the love of God. What's done in obedience to Him will lay up treasure in heaven.

. . . And Never Give Up!

Finishing the race is never easy and many people give up when the going gets tougher than they would like it to be. So, as we come to the end of our book on *Living Life God's Way* I want to use these final paragraphs to urge you to consider Jesus – who didn't give up, because of His love for you and for me – and to consider your calling and destiny in God. Resolve never to give up living the Christian life and serving the God who loved you so much that He sent Jesus to be your Savior.

When I met Jackie Pullinger in Hong Kong, I was privileged to be talking to a lady who never took No for an answer, if God had already said Yes! The record of her achievements under God is almost beyond belief. She gave herself to serving the people of the walled city in the days before it was demolished. She counted the cost and still said, Yes. Countless thousands of people, many of them drug addicts without hope in this world, discovered Jesus and discovered healing through her ministry.

When I read of the perseverance of William Carey in India, and the extraordinary adventures of the hundreds of pioneering missionaries who followed in William Carey's footsteps, I'm lost in admiration. They counted the cost and still said, Yes. I am praying there'll be a library in heaven, where I'll be able to read every one of their stories and adventures.

And I am praying also that in that heavenly library I will be able to pick up a volume telling me of your personal story. In the letters to the seven churches in the book of Revelation (chapters 2 and 3) there are some wonderful promises given to the different church fellowships Jesus is writing to through the pen of John. But the condition attached to each of the promises in all seven letters is simply *"To him who overcomes"* or *"overcomes and endures to the end."*

These precious promises are not for those who only began well, but for those who *began and finished* well. We all have to begin, but it is only those who overcome and endure to the end who will be the inheritors of the greatest blessings. I pray that this book will have helped you on the journey of life and that you will be one of those who receives the reward of an overcomer.

Summary

Life is a race – not a race in which we're running against others, but a race in which we're seeking to achieve everything God has laid out for us in His plans and purposes for our life. Each of us has a destiny to fulfill. It's only through obedience to Him who fulfilled His destiny, that we will experience the joy of knowing the power of the resurrection in our lives and ministries.

About the Author

Peter Horrobin is the Founder and International Director of Ellel Ministries. Ellel Ministries International was first established in 1986 as a ministry of healing in the north-west of England. The work is now (in 2016) established in over thirty different countries and students who have trained with Ellel Ministries are working in every continent and in well over forty different countries.

Peter was born in 1943 in Bolton, Lancashire, and was later brought up in Blackburn, also in the north of England. His parents gave him a firm Christian foundation for life with a strong evangelical emphasis. His early grounding in the scriptures was to equip him for future ministry.

After graduating from Oxford University with a degree in Chemistry, he spent a number of years in College and University lecturing, before leaving the academic environment for the world of business where he founded a series of successful publishing and bookselling companies.

In his twenties he started to restore a vintage sports car (an *Alvis Speed 20*), but discovered that its chassis was bent. As he looked at the broken vehicle, wondering if it could ever be repaired, he sensed God asking him a question, *"You could restore this broken car, but I can restore broken lives. Which is more important?"* It was obvious that broken lives were more important than broken cars and so the beginnings of a vision for restoring people was birthed in his heart.

A few years later, he was asked to try and help a person who had been sexually abused. Through this experience God opened up to him the vision for the healing ministry. He prayed daily into this vision until, in 1986, God brought it into being at Ellel Grange, a country house just outside the City of Lancaster. Many Christian leaders affirmed the vision and gave it their support.

Since then a hallmark of Peter's ministry has been his willingness to step out in faith and see God move to fulfil His promises, often in remarkable ways.

Under Peter's leadership, with his wife Fiona, the world-wide teaching and ministry team has seen God move dramatically in many people's lives to bring salvation, hope, healing and deliverance. Together they teach and minister on many different aspects of healing and discipleship.

The work is a faith ministry, depending totally on donations and income from training courses for maintaining and extending the work.

Outside of Ellel Ministries, Peter was the originator and one of the compilers of the amazingly successful and popular **Mission Praise**, now in its 30th Anniversary Edition. It was originally compiled for Billy Graham's *Mission England* in 1984.

He is also an enthusiast for fishing and classic cars. His **Complete Catalogue of British Cars**, which was first published in 1975, has long been a standard reference work on the history and technical specification of every model of every make of British car manufactured between 1895 and 1975! During his years in academic life he also wrote and edited books of specialist technical interest about different aspects of building science and technology.

Peter wrote the teaching contained within the online training programme *Ellel 365*. This is about to be relaunched, both on-line and in book form, as *Journey to Freedom*. This 365-part programme provides daily input to those seeking healing, training and an understanding of what it means to be a follower and disciple of Jesus. Many have testified to the life-transforming blessing it has brought to their lives.

**For details about the current worldwide activities of
Ellel Ministries International please go to
www.ellel.org.**

Other Books by Peter Horrobin

available from Sovereign World at
www.sovereignworld.com

Forgiveness – God's Master Key

Forgiveness is key to the restoration of our relationship with God and to healing from the consequences of hurtful, damaging human relationships. From the cross, Jesus prayed these dramatic words to God, "Father, forgive them, for they do not know what they are doing." Learning to forgive others is the beginning of a lifetime's adventure with God – it really is the most powerful prayer on earth!

Paperback 110 pages ISBN 978-1-852405-02-1

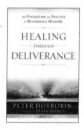

Healing Through Deliverance

The Foundation and Practice of Deliverance Ministry

In this ground-breaking book, Peter Horrobin draw on his thirty years of experience of ministry to lay out the biblical basis for healing through deliverance. He provides safe guidelines for ministry, helps the reader identify demonic entry points and teaches how we can be delivered and healed from the effects of demonic power. His prayer for the reader is that their commitment to Christ will be deepened and that they will respond afresh to God's call to heal the broken-hearted and set the captives free.

Hardback 630 pages ISBN 978-1-852404-98-7

The Truth Stick

A Parable for Adults and Children

This is a truly enchanting story of Ratty, Mole and Badger and the adventures they have discovering the amazing secrets that lie hidden in Wild Winters Wood! Ratty's question "What is truth?" reveals the answers every child needs to know. Whether young or old, you will be delighted with this refreshing tale.

Hardback 128 pages ISBN 0-9546380-1-8

Journey to Freedom (Coming Soon)

Personal Transformation – One Day at a Time

Book 1 *Building on the Rock*
ISBN 978-1-852407-42-1
Book 2 *God, Me and the Enemy*
ISBN 978-1-852407-57-5
Book 3 *Our Faithful God*
ISBN 978-1-852407-72-8
Book 4 *Jesus – Our Living Hope*
ISBN 978-1-852407-61-2
Book 5 *Jesus – Healer and Deliverer*
ISBN 978-1-852407-96-4
Book 6 *Dying to Live!*
ISBN 978-1-852407-70-4
Book 7 *God's Vision for My Life*
ISBN 978-1-852407-85-8

*Each volume in the series is a large format flexi-cover of
between 280–320 pages, with room on each page for personal
notes and comments.*

Journey to Freedom was originally published online as a
daily journey of faith and understanding. Many hundreds
of readers in all the major countries of the world gave
testimony to the blessing of the teaching in their lives.
Now, for the first time, Peter's systematic teaching is
being made available in a seven-book series of volumes
containing a total of 260 life-transforming chapters.

> *"It is personal and practical, pastoral and prophetic,
> encouraging and educating, appealing and revealing. The
> illustrations and stories and testimonies relate biblical
> explanation to spiritual experience. It is Christ-centered,
> Holy Spirit-empowered and inspired. I love it! I need it! I'm
> going to use it! So should you!"*

Pastor Stuart McAlpine
Christ Our Shepherd Church, Capitol Hill,
Washington D.C.

The Parables of Harris

Lessons from the Real-Life Adventures of a Black Labrador

From the founders of Ellel Ministries International comes this amusing and entertaining book about Harris, their black Labrador. *"From the day Harris came home our lives were changed for ever! From the moment he put his first huge paw over our threshold, and took control of the home, we knew we were in for an adventure!"* And his adventurous exploits have become modern-day parables of life.
Paperback 128 pages ISBN 0-9546380-0-X

Healing from the consequences of Accident, Shock and Trauma

Peter Horrobin

Traumatic events leave a scar on broken lives. Unhealed trauma is one of the primary reasons why some people do not easily heal from the consequences of accidents or sudden shocks. This ground-breaking book is the culmination of thirty years of experience praying for such people. Peter carefully explains what trauma can do to people and how to pray for healing. This foundational teaching has been instrumental in bringing permanent healing to people all over the world. An essential manual for those who regularly pray for people – a life-transforming handbook for those who are struggling themselves with unresolved and unhealed issues – including the consequences of shock and injuries sustained in the military.
Paperback 176 pages, ISBN 9781852407438

Appendix

About Ellel Ministries
www.ellel.org

Our Vision

Ellel Ministries is a non-denominational Christian Mission Organization with a vision to resource and equip the Church by welcoming people, teaching them about the Kingdom of God and healing those in need (Luke 9:11).

Our Mission

Our mission is to fulfill the above vision throughout the world, as God opens the doors, in accordance with the Great Commission of Jesus and the calling of the Church to proclaim the Kingdom of God by preaching the good news, healing the broken-hearted and setting the captives free. We are, therefore, committed to evangelism, healing, deliverance, discipleship and training. The particular scriptures on which our mission is founded are Isaiah 61:1–7; Matthew 28:18–20; Luke 9:1–2; 9:11; Ephesians 4:12; 2 Timothy 2:2.

Our Basis of Faith

God is a Trinity. God the Father loves all people. God the Son, Jesus Christ, is Savior and Healer, Lord and King. God the Holy Spirit indwells Christians and imparts the dynamic power by which they are enabled to continue Christ's ministry. The Bible is the divinely inspired authority in matters of faith, doctrine and conduct, and is the basis for teaching.

Ellel Ministries International
Ellel Grange,
Ellel,
Lancaster, LA2 0HN
United Kingdom

Sovereign World Ltd

For details of new titles
and information about all Sovereign World's books,
please go to:
www.sovereignworld.com

or write to the company at the headquarters address:

Sovereign World Ltd.,

P.O.Box 784,
Ellel,
Lancaster,
LA1 9DA
United Kingdom

Or send us an email to:
info@sovereignworld.com

Most books are also available in e-book format and can be purchased online.

Would You Join With Us To Bless the Nations?

At the Sovereign World Trust, our mandate and passion is to send books, like the one you've just read, to *faithful leaders who can equip others* (2 Tim 2:2).

The 'Good News' is that in all of the poorest nations we reach, the Kingdom of God is growing in an accelerated way but, to further this Great Commission work, the Pastors and Leaders in these countries need good teaching resources in order to provide sound Biblical doctrine to their flock, their future generations and especially new converts.

If you could donate a copy of this or other titles from Sovereign World Ltd, you will be helping to supply much-needed resources to Pastors and Leaders in many countries.

Contact us for more information on (+44)(0)1732 851150 or visit our website www.sovereignworldtrust.org.uk

> *"I have all it takes to further my studies. Sovereign is making it all possible for me"*
>
> **Rev. Akfred Keyas – Kenya**

> *"My ministry is rising up gradually since I have been teaching people from these books"*
>
> **Pastor John Obaseki – Nigeria**